LAST-CHANCE CHILDREN

LAST-CHANCE CHILDREN

Growing Up with Older Parents

Monica Morris

COLUMBIA UNIVERSITY PRESS
NEW YORK   1988

Library of Congress Cataloging-in-Publication Data
Morris, Monica B., 1928–
    Last-chance children
    Growing up with older parents
    Bibliography: p.
    1. Parenting—United States. 2. Parent and child—
United States. 3. Middle age—United States.
4. Childbirth in middle age—United States. 5. Parents,
Aged—United States—Family relationships. I. Title.
HQ755.8.M65   1988   306.8'74   87-27845
ISBN 0-231-06694-5

Columbia University Press
New York   Guilford, Surrey
Copyright © 1988 Monica Morris

Book design by Ken Venezio

Contents

Prologue

Deferred parenting is a current social trend. While overall birthrate has increased only slightly in recent years, births among women over thirty years old have increased by more than 35 percent.

Writers have been quick to notice this phenomenon and books and articles written for and about women having babies "late" in life have proliferated. Nothing much, however, has yet been written about the possible effects on the *children* of being born to older parents. Will they face problems not experienced by other children?

The idea for *Last-Chance Children* came from the interest and enthusiasm generated when I was doing research for an article on the subject for the *Los Angeles Times*. Requests for interviews following publication of the piece were from now adult late-born children, eager to tell how much they appreciated their childhood years and to express the love and affection they felt for their older parents; others were from those who wanted to release their resentments against their older parents and to express their disapproval of contemporary late childbearers.

Still other responses were from people who were, themselves, relatively late starters at parenting and many of whose letters expressed anger that the subject had been raised at all. "Older parents may well be better, more patient, parents than younger ones," one older parent wrote. And another, whose letter was published in the *Times*, asked: "Though some children of older parents may have feared loss, I wonder if they would have preferred the alternative, no life at all!"

As the *Times* article had made the same point as did the first writer above, that many people feel much more capable as parents in their thirties and forties than they did in their twenties, and as nowhere was any criticism leveled against couples choosing late parenting or any suggestion made that such people should resist the temptation to procreate, one might see such responses as somewhat overreactive, even defensive!

Indeed, parents of late-born children do sometimes seem to protest too much, to insist that late childbearing is the preferred pattern of family life, and are not eager to hear anything that may give cause for the slightest doubt. Guests on a Phil Donahue program on late-parenting—late fathers, primarily, although some late mothers were among the studio audience—waxed ecstatic about the joys of fatherhood and how much better they could appreciate their infants, now that some of the pressures of the rat race have eased, now that they can take time to play with their babies and participate in their rearing.

This trend, if it can be so termed, for fathers to share some of the childrearing tasks can only be applauded. Research for this book indicates that late-born children whose parents were generous with themselves and their leisure time remember their childhood years with more affection than those whose parents were less involved. This might, of course, apply to *any* children, regardless of their parents' ages and, indeed, much in this book will speak to all parents desiring their children's well-being and sense of security.

Other insights, though, are specific to children of older parents, for even those who describe their childhood years as idyllic have some reservations about the double generation gap between their parents and themselves. One young man of twenty, among others, whose love for and loyalty toward his older parents allowed him to speak only glowingly of them and all they had done for him, unhesitatingly responded "No!" when asked if he planned late parenting for himself or would recommend it as a pattern. A woman of twenty-five, however, as yet unmarried, said she would start her family late. "There's so much I want to do first," she said. Then, voicing the frustration of many contemporary single women by the seeming lack of commitment to marriage by men of their generation, she added, "Of course, first I've got to find someone to have children *with.*"

About one half of those interviewed for this study expressed either generally positive feelings about being "late" babies or felt unaffected by it—"I never really thought about it much." The others though, felt their parents' ages were significant, that such ages affected their lives deeply and usually negatively. Given that many couples are choosing to delay parenting, what can they do to assure that their ages have the least negative impact on their children? Are there steps they can take to help their children lead relatively happy, untroubled childhood years?

Some answers to these questions lie in what people who are themselves children of older parents say about their experiences, the particulars of their lives revealed in their interviews.

After the first few interview tapes were transcribed, patterns began to emerge. Certain commonalities ran through the tapes like somber or brightly colored threads. Rather than presenting the same statements repeatedly throughout the book, chapters are presented by themes. The sample is not large but it appears to be fairly representative of two major points of view about having older parents. The comments, memories, and experiences the interviewees expressed very rapidly fell into clear categories. In fact, the responses became so repetitious, different people not only making the same kinds of observations but often using almost the same words, that I initially stopped interviewing after the first eighteen subjects' comments had been collected. Later, I added four more interviewees, again recruited as before, to satisfy myself that the sample was, indeed, fairly representative. Little new was added, the further four subjects voicing very similar sentiments to those offered previously.

The twenty-two children of older parents interviewed for this book were born and reared in many different states, including California, Michigan, Missouri, Oklahoma, Texas, and New York; one was British-born. All but one were living in California when interviewed, some as long-term residents, some as newcomers. The one out-of-state subject lived in Arkansas and was interviewed by telephone. They are real people; only their names are fictitious and some unimportant but identifying personal characteristics have been altered to protect their privacy.

The interviewees ranged in age from seventeen to fifty-four years. For most, their mothers' ages ranged from thirty-five to forty-six and their fathers' ages ranged from thirty-five to fifty-two when their babies were born. Exceptions to this were the mothers of Rebecca Johnson and Priscilla Banks, both of whom were only thirty-one years old when those children were born. "But she always *seemed* so much older than my friends' mothers," both Rebecca and Priscilla insisted. Seven in the sample were late-born *only* children, the others were the last in families with two or more children. Many were "caboose" babies, with a substantial number of years between their births and the births of the children before them: eleven and seventeen years, in one case; seven, twelve, sixteen, and twenty years in another; thirteen years; ten, fourteen, and fifteen years; ten, sixteen, and nineteen years; and five and eight years in others. In Rebecca Johnson's case only, there was a gap of only nineteen months between her and her older brother. And in only one case was the child of older parents, Janet Spruce, the middle child of three adopted children, with eight years between Janet and her older brother and only two years between Janet and her younger sister.

One child, Jean Smythe, was born to a single mother. Stephen

Grey also grew up in a single parent home; he does not remember his father, who died when Stephen was three years old. A number of others interviewed were left fatherless while still young, in their teens.

The twenty-two people who participated in this inquiry constitute a "snowball sample" or a contingency sample, as it is sometimes termed. When I first expressed an interest in knowing more about the feelings of children born late in their parents' lives, a colleague suggested an acquaintance of his as a possible subject. In turn, professional associates and friends suggested names, and interviewees themselves suggested other late-born children. Students in my classes knew of now-adult children of older parents, one of my students asking colleagues at her workplace, a local large office complex, if they knew of any candidates for interviewing. The criterion for eligibility was that each subject's parents have been at least thirty-five years old at the time of the subject's birth. I had no way of knowing, nor did I wish to know in advance of interviewing them, whether these now-adult children had been happy or unhappy as children or whether they had strong emotions, negative or positive, about their parents' ages.

The interviews lasted from one to three hours. Some were face-to-face, some were telephone interviews. I used a tape recorder as well as written notes to ensure word-for-word accuracy of subjects' statements. After noting factual information, such as sex and age of the subject, age of parents when the subject was born, place in the family, ages and sexes of siblings, I asked nondirective questions that encouraged free, wide-ranging responses, sometimes interjecting, "Tell me more about that," or "How did you feel about that?" to bring focus to the often rambling reminiscences. Toward the end of the interviews, I asked for a summary of what the subjects perceived as the advantages and disadvantages of being born late in their parents' lives; I also asked if, given such a choice, they would choose to have children late themselves, and would they recommend late-parenting to their friends.

This inquiry rests upon, and draws from, a theoretical framework I have elsewhere termed "creative sociology" (1977). Similar approaches also inform the work of some anthropologists, social psychologists, and other social scientists. Creative sociology, which includes phenomenology, symbolic interaction, and ethnomethodology, is concerned with understanding events and issues from the point of view of the people, the subjects, involved, rather than with imposing the observer's view of what is going on in the situation. To achieve this kind of understanding, the researcher tries to start without any preconceived notions about what might, or might not, be found. No hypotheses guide the work but, in the course of the research, patterns may emerge that allow some generalizations to be drawn. In turn, these may suggest hypotheses that can then be tested or, as Glaser and Strauss (1967) have indicated, theory may be discovered from the data.

I am indebted to many more people than I can name here for their help and encouragement while preparing this book. Most especially, my thanks go to my dear friends and colleagues Fred Lynch, Patricia Cole, Joyce and Marvin Scott, Francesca Alexander and, of course, and as always, to Manning. My appreciation, also, to Louise Waller at Columbia University Press for her unflagging enthusiasm and support. And to all those who invested their time, patience, thought, and emotional energy in speaking out, thank you. The beneficiaries will be the children.

LAST-CHANCE CHILDREN

1

Late-Parenting: Who Speaks for the Children?

Being the child of an older mother may be the most significant fact of my early life.—Jean, born when her mother was forty-three

Being the child of older parents was so painful to me, I would never be an older parent, myself. I could not do that to a child.—Margaret, born when her parents were nearly forty-two

In the 1980s, following the trend of the 1970s, older women are having babies in record numbers. Around one million babies each year, 150,000 of them first-born babies, are being born to mothers aged thirty to forty-four, of a total of about three and a half million babies. This fact has been much publicized in the popular media: Candace Bergen, we learn from the press, delivered her first child at thirty-nine; her husband was fifty-three—ten years older than my father was when his first grandchild was born. Bette Midler had her first child at forty, and Goldie Hawn also at forty, gave birth to her third baby. Kurt Vonnegut, following a similar late-parenting trend for men, fathered a baby daughter when he was sixty, and Dr. Robert Butler, a specialist in gerontology, was fifty-two when his daughter was born.

The reasons for the increase in births to older parents have been well documented and are given here as the background against which to examine a much less investigated topic: What does it mean to be *child* of older parents? Do the children of older parents face problems that other children are spared? Are they embarrassed to have parents who are older than the parents of their friends? Are *only* children of older parents especially disadvantaged or, rather, especially advantaged, compared to children who must share resources with their siblings? And how does the "caboose" baby fare, the one born several years after other children in the family? Can parents in their fifties, even in their sixties, remember and understand the turmoil of adolescence as well as parents in their thirties and forties do? Are children of older parents driven to achieve more than children of younger parents? Do children resent their older parents? Do they fear death—the death of their parents—more than do other children?

Given the current trend toward deferred childbearing, these questions should be asked. The answers can only help those considering having babies—and serve as guides to older parents in rearing those babies.

Why So Many Older Mothers?

The children of post-World War II, the "baby-boom" babies, with more years of education and higher personal and professional aspirations than any previous generation, delayed childbearing. This tendency to postpone parenthood, even to postpone marriage, was encouraged by several powerful social changes. New methods of birth control allowed sexual intercourse to become entirely recreational rather than procreational; the new feminism legitimated freedom for sexual expression and experimentation outside of wedlock; and women began to feel that, if they wished, they could exercise the same option as men to make a profession rather than a family the central consuming interest in their lives. With the passing of time, however, and as large numbers of baby-boom babies reach the age of thirty each year—and then move through their thirties—a sense of urgency has become almost palpable. If they wait much longer, these women may have lost all chance of ever having babies of their own. Even militant feminists, who deplored the "oppression" implied by child-bearing and childrearing, are having second thoughts as they approach, and pass, their thirtieth birthdays. Paula Cizmar, in a *Mother Jones* article published in 1979 writes: "On my next birthday I will be thirty and I don't want to be a casualty of the war between my politics and my biological clock."

So now, women in their middle and late thirties are hurrying to have babies before their biological clocks stop ticking. Overall birthrate has risen hardly at all, but first births among women over thirty years old have jumped by over 35 percent in recent years, with the trend sharpest among urban professional women. In 1981, for instance, the mean age of new mothers at Chicago's Northwestern Memorial Hospital was reported to be thirty-three years, and demand forced New York's Maternity Center to raise the maximum age for nonhospital deliveries from thirty-four to thirty-nine for first-time mothers. Further, one Westside Los Angeles hospital found that the largest age category for women giving birth in its delivery center in 1986 was thirty-five to forty-two.

"Caboose" babies, too—arriving perhaps ten years or more after the previous child—are being born not only to parents who want another child before it is too late, but also to the divorced and remarried woman who must act quickly if she is to have a child fathered by her new husband.

Who Speaks for the Children?

While a fairly balanced view is given about the costs and benefits of later childbearing to women in such books as *Up Against the Clock*, by Marilyn Fabe and Norma Wikler, and *Sooner or Later*, by Pamela Daniels and Kathy Weingarten, little attention has yet been paid to the costs and benefits to the children of these older parents, children who will always have "elderly" parents, nearly as old, perhaps, as many of their friends' *grandparents*.

The new parents of these "buds of autumn" are likely to insist that their offspring can only benefit from the affluence of their homes, their opportunities for the best education, the best of everything that money can buy, and the loving attention of parents who truly wanted them, longed for them, and welcomed them into the world.

Dora Sernat (whom I interviewed earlier in the study but who is not, herself, the child of older parents) has, at age thirty-six, a new marriage and a new baby boy. She feels much better prepared for motherhood now than when her two older sons were born. The two boys, aged thirteen and fourteen, live with their father, from whom Sernat was divorced when the boys were small. Until recently, she took full responsibility for their care.

"I can't tell you what a terrible mother I was as a young woman," she says. "At twenty-one and twenty-two, I was really just a kid and the children had to grow up with me, financially, emotionally, intellectually, and I couldn't provide very much direction, very much authority, to them. I feel I can with the [new] baby. And the fact of having more money helps, and being able to pay for a very stable situation for him, where somebody lives in and his caretaking is all in the home. He never has to leave ... he's not bandied about from pillar to post ... I'm not a nervous wreck, which I always was, just because there was so much work to do. I was always with the other two, either going to school and taking care of them, or working and taking care of them, which meant their schedule had to conform to mine, and mine was just rushing from dawn to dusk, really, trying to get them to a babysitter, and pick them up, and if the babysitter quit, finding another one. You know ... all of those problems ... and never having enough (money) ... and also feeling guilty about leaving them with babysitters, which I don't anymore. I feel like he's just fine. He's a terrifically well-adjusted child. Something I didn't know then, but I do know now, is that he will be fine as long as I am fine, emotionally, and he is not fine if I'm upset."

Sernat, who holds an interesting, well-paying job with a utility company, says she doesn't have, and never did have, the patience for twenty-four-hours-a-day child care. The weekends with her baby are enough to leave her "shot." "But," she says, "this is a function of being older and wiser and accepting the fact that I can't do that." Being able to afford resident care for her child leaves her free, she says, both for stimulating work, and to enjoy the time she spends with her baby.

Several studies indicate that an infant's development is directly related to the level of the mother's education, among other maternal characteristics. Mothers with more education tend to talk more to their babies, provide more interesting toys, and are more effective teachers, offering help and using praise rather than criticism when teaching (see Clarke-Stewart et al. 1985:85). Like Sernat, the over-thirty mother of today tends to be better educated and more affluent than ever before. A U.S. Census Bureau study published in 1983 found that 51 percent of the women over thirty who gave birth in 1982 had completed one year or more of college, 43 percent lived in families with incomes of over $25,000 annually, 41 percent were employed, and 31 percent were employed as professionals.

By contrast, only 26 percent of women giving birth in their twenties had completed a year or more of college; 21 percent lived in families with annual incomes of $25,000 or more. Thirty-four percent were employed but only 14 percent were employed as professionals.

The older working mother, especially the older first-time mother, is generally financially well-off and, in shopping for herself and her baby, is willing and able to pay for quality, convenience, and style.

Newspapers, magazines, and television features report the boom in baby-related industries: couturier clothes for tiny tots, including designer label diapers; elegant maternity wear; and expensive day schools for babies as young as six weeks.

Is late-parenting merely a selfish whim?

More women are postponing childbearing until after age 30 when they are "more mature, more settled, more psychologically and emotionally able to raise kids and cope with them better."—Dr. Atef Moawad, chief of obstetrics University of Chicago Medical Center, 1984

These babies are conceived . . . with no thought for the future. Their conception is merely the next step—perhaps the Ultimate Experience—in their mothers' quest for fulfillment.—Naomi Munsen, *Commentary*, April 1981

In any discussion about older parents, one of the above views is likely to prevail. Mothers who postpone childbearing are either selfless, caring people, sensible enough to give proper thought to the economics of childrearing and to wait until they are established in a career and are financially stable, *or* such women are driven only by the current cultural dogma:
"These [older career women]," writes Naomi Munsen, "have had their share of cocaine and caviar; they've shot the rapids in a canoe and roller-boogied till 5 a.m; they've done the Caribbean and the Aegaen; they've kept clean for Gene and dressed for success; they've tried the new sexuality and the new celibacy. Now they are 'into' pregnancy."
Whether one feels some empathy with older women having babies now, and tries to understand the social, economic, and political contexts in which they must make difficult choices or, alternatively, takes Munsen's harsher view that such women are thinking only of their own need, the fact remains: older women are having babies.
Several books and dozens of articles have appeared, attempting to allay women's fears about the health hazards of late childbearing. Amniocentesis and ultrasound are encouraged for older pregnant women: amniocentesis, the drawing and analysis of a sample of the amniotic fluid surrounding the fetus,

can help discern chromosomal abnormalities—more likely to increase with the mother's age—thus allowing the expectant mother to decide for or against abortion, should serious genetic problems be discovered.

Voices become especially strident whenever abortion enters the debate on the pros and cons of postponed parenting. Even some of those in favor of assuring the birth of as healthy, as genetically sound, a child as possible, particularly given the means to detect flaws in the fetus, are a little uneasy that amniocentesis is performed in the fourth or fifth month of pregnancy and that, therefore, termination must be delayed until well into the second trimester. For the sake of all concerned, the condition of the fetus would, ideally, be known within weeks of conception when abortion is far less traumatic.

When an anti-abortionist also feels that the decision to bear a "last-chance" child is merely a selfish whim, words on paper are etched in acid: "amniocentesis . . . (I)f the fetus is found to have a debilitating defect, it is aborted," writes Naomi Munsen, "thus saving the parents—and society—the agony and expense of supporting what has come to be seen by all right-thinking people as a life 'not worth living.' . . . For it is in the essence of this new style that there should be no need for anyone to bear or raise a less than perfect baby."

The facts, as presented by Arthur J. Salisbury, M.D., of the March of Dimes Birth Defects Foundation, are that "between ninety-five and ninety-seven percent of women who undergo amniocentesis are reassured that the condition they are concerned about is not present in the fetus. Others have shown a dramatic decrease in abortions among families 'at risk' because of specific disorders since the introduction of prenatal diagnosis." Other advances in medical technology, besides providing prenatal diagnosis, even allow some kinds of surgery in utero, making late childbearing safer than ever before.

Much of this advice and information is directed to the educated, professional woman. In some cases, this woman is unmarried but chooses to bear a child and rear it alone—for her own fulfillment, perhaps, or because she feels she has an abundance of life's good things to offer a child. Again, new options are open to her, including conception through artificial insemination, should she prefer no direct physical contact with her child's father. Popular movies often achieve their box-office success because they so accurately reflect societal change or societal *angst*. In a poignant scene in *The Big Chill*, which relates the stories of six baby-boom babies now in their thirties who had been in the same class at the University of Michigan, Meg, complaining to her old friend, says that she has been dating for twenty years, and she's getting tired of it. She's weary of discovering that all the men she meets are either married or gay. She's not even sure she wants a husband any more, but what she knows she does want is a baby. And she is determined to have one before it is too late, even though she is not married. Meg's condition matches that of countless "aging" young single women among the baby-boom population who outnumber available marriage partners. And as each year passes for a woman, so the pool of marriageable men grows smaller.

With her remarks about the pleasure of childrearing, now she can afford a resident child-carer, Sernat unwittingly hurls herself directly onto the daggers drawn by those who see the deferral of childbearing as a selfish whim. The term "quality time," referring to the perhaps brief but intense interaction a working mother has with her baby, has been ridiculed as mere rationalization by those who believe that *all* of a mother's time should be spent with her young children. Listen to members of the audience of some of the Phil Donahue Shows, for instance, for "middle-America's" disparaging views of the woman who delegates care of her young to others. This disparagement persists, despite the rapid increase in the female labor force since the 1950s, and the "promise" to women, especially in college, that they can, and should, compete with men in management, medicine, law, or any of the other professions.

Naomi Munson's pen pours pure vitriol onto the page when she writes about child care:

The truth . . . is that while *having* babies is very much the thing, taking the energy to raise them properly is still definitely declasse . . . . It seems not to occur to their parents that after the amnio is done, after the classes are over, after the movies of the delivery have been developed, there will have been brought into the world a new and helpless baby, in need of constant and ungrudging attention. Faced with this reality, the new-style mothers and fathers appear to be fleeing from it as if from the plague.

From many parents' position, though, "quality" child care, far from being detrimental to their children's development will, in fact, enhance their social skills. The evidence so far, however, does not indicate that children in day-care centers or nursery schools are significantly advantaged or disadvantaged, compared to children whose early years are spent with their mothers.

More Views on Late-Parenting

Paula Parrish, a vice-principal of an elementary school, also a new mother, a first-time mother at thirty-six, sees many parents and children together during her working day and is particularly alert to differences between younger and older parents in their interactions with their offspring. She notices that parents who are "older than usual" tend to be more "uptight" with their children, to place more restrictions on them, and to have, she says, "a more conservative" approach to childrearing.

"The age gap is probably not important at first," Seymour says, "but it may become more significant when the children are teenagers. We late-starting parents will have to guard against becoming old fogies to our children."

And while parents may speak positively about the effects on their children of being born to mature, stable, older adults, experts such as Dr. Ruth Neubauer, past president of the New

York Association of Marriage and Family Therapy, are likely to temper optimism with caution.

According to Neubauer, older parents have more life experiences behind them and so are generally more sensitive and receptive to their children's needs and more likely to give up personal satisfactions than are younger parents, because they have already had time to experience them. The first, or only, child of an over-forty parent is often a high achiever because he or she receives a lot of parental attention and stimulation. Such a child may develop verbal skills at an early age, but a great deal of parental expectation and pressure may be a burden on the youngster, especially if he or she feels unable to live up to those expectations. Being overprotective is another concern. Older parents are often more restrictive, as the school vice-principal has noted above, and as is corroborated by Neubauer, and are more concerned with possible dangers than may be beneficial to the child. Dr. Iris Kern, though, a professor of social welfare, who has studied older mothers, emphasises the positive side of late-parenting. She is quoted in the *New York Times* as finding older parents especially attentive to their children. They "expose them to more varied experiences and are less likely to divorce."

Before this study was completed, little information, positive or negative, has been available about how children are affected by having parents who are older than is "normal." In Daniels and Weingarten's *Sooner or Later,* parenting is viewed primarily as "one of the major growth-promoting experiences of adulthood," with the emphasis on the parents' decision to have a child either early or late in their life together and what that decision means to *them*. The authors do point out the greater willingness of older couples—forty years old and older—contemplating a first baby to consider aborting a defective fetus. "(This) reflected a sharp awareness of the liability of their age and the long-run implications of this for parenthood of a disabled child." "Who would take care of the child if 'something happened' to Mike and me?" one woman quoted by

Daniels and Weingarten asked. "I wouldn't have *been* in that position ... if I'd been ... younger." The question of who would care for the child if the parents died seems not to have been addressed about a "normal" baby. In *Up Against the Clock* too, Fabe and Wikler address dozens of issues of importance to older women contemplating having a baby. Among them are:

Will pregnancy and motherhood affect the way my professional competence is perceived and evaluated?

How will having both a career and a child affect my relationship to my mate?

Can I predict how much conflict and stress I might have if I combine children with my career?

What are the psychological and social ramifications of being an 'old' new mother?

And, although the single woman is asked to consider the psychological risks, the social stigma, for the child, and whether a child needs a father in the home, the broader issue is not addressed: what might be the consequences to the children of the choice, by both married and single women, to defer childbearing until substantially later than is considered the optimal time?

Why So Few Studies of Children of Older Parents?

The rationale for the omission is that we cannot know how this generation of late babies will be affected, and that to go back to previous generations for investigation would not be fruitful: only in our era, it has been suggested, are women delayng children and only now are they combining childrearing with demanding careers. The experiences of children born to older parents thirty, forty, or more years ago will have been very different from the experiences of babies born in the 1970s and 1980s.

The notion of the uniqueness of this generation of "late" babies seems to prevail. Several older mothers and fathers interviewed for preliminary work for this study indicated that, because of the increase in births among older women, their children, unlike "late" babies of the past, will have a peer group. "All our friends of the same age are having babies," one new father, a professional man in his mid-thirties said. "And they'll all grow up together. Their peers will all be in the same boat; older parents will be the norm for them." Dora Sernat, too, feels her new baby will have more of a peer group than "late" babies of the past. Both these parents see late childbearing in previous generations as more unusual than it is today.

The current "baby boomlet" among older mothers, however, is not a unique phenomenon. The United States saw a similar increase in births among older women at the beginning of the post-World War II baby boom, helping, in part, to power that boom.

Census data show fertility in the United States at an all-time low from the mid 1920s through to the 1940s. During the Depression, many couples delayed both marriage and childbearing, and the war, following closely on the heels of the Depression, separated husbands from wives. When the war ended and the men came home, these families hurried to have babies. During the period following the war, while overall fertility rose, the sharpest fertility gains were among women above the age of thirty-five.

The children of these older mothers were not alone; they did have peers. Charles Finch was born in 1946 to a mother of thirty-eight, a father of forty-three. He remembers that the parents of several of his childhood friends were in their forties and fifties, as were his own mother and father. This group of "children" can be compared to those born from the mid-1970s and through the 1980s. Although these youngsters will have peers, they will still represent a minority among children of their own age. Most children will have young parents. And those born when their mothers were over thirty-five, although they, too, will have some peers, will represent a relatively small percentage of all youngsters. First-born children (who will probably also be only children) will be even less representative. First-born babies born to women aged thirty to forty-four years (the true deferrers) between June 1981 and June 1982 numbered approximately 150,000—a large number, warranting study, but a small percentage of the nearly 3.5 million babies born during that year.

It is true that childbirth out of wedlock was not as socially accepted in the 1940s as it is now, but women—professional women—did have babies and did rear them without husbands. Jean Smythe was born to such a woman in 1946.

No two generations are alike; for each, unique economic, societal, and political conditions and events make for different perceptions of the world and leave different scars. Even so, the experiences of the generation of the recent past may be helpful in understanding the present generation when the members of both share a specific characteristic, that of being born toward the end of their mothers' childbearing years. Jean Smythe says that being the only child of an older mother may be the most significant fact of her early life. The ways in which this fact was significant for her, and for other children of older parents, may give some insights into what "late" children of any generation feel and may help avoid problems possibly not foreseen by today's older parents.

Saying Is Doing

The "children" speaking out in the following pages speak with their own voices; they tell their own stories, from their own memories. Memory, we know, is imperfect; it plays tricks. And stories become distorted with time and, sometimes, in the telling. The words, though, make the reality. What people say, and how they say it, shapes their social world. Saying is doing, and in talking about their older parents, some of the people interviewed began articulating feelings they appeared not to have acknowledged before. Once the words were said, the deed was done. The anger, the resentment, and the guilt they felt about expressing those sentiments, or the gratitude, the appreciation—all of these were real.

What people say also tells something about social convention—what admissions are acceptable and what can be written only if the speaker's identity is concealed. Some of the interviews were taped face-to-face, with the tape-recorder in full view, others were conducted by telephone, with the recording instrument beeping every few seconds as a constant reminder that words were being committed to tape. Even so, when some of those interviewed read the transcripts, they were surprised, even shocked, by how much they had revealed, and asked that they remain anonymous in the published work. Mostly they felt shame, they said, and guilt, about what they had said. "I really *loved* my mother," one respondent, Marilyn Henry, insisted. "and I wouldn't want people who knew her, and who know me, to know that I had those other feelings."

Experiences can be understood only through the words of those who have lived them. Even if those words do not represent "truth," they do tell what people *felt* was the truth.

George Orwell, in "Such, such were the joys...", his recollections of his schooldays, writes of the real difficulty of knowing what a child really feels or thinks. "A child which appears happy may actually be suffering horrors which it cannot or or will not reveal."

Marilyn Henry, both the only child of an older mother and, herself, the mother of a "late" child, is sometimes able to discern the real worries underlying her little daughter's words. She remembers the same worries from her own childhood and recalls her inability, then, to say exactly what she felt. "I didn't want to hurt my mother's feelings," she says. Her special understanding helps her anticipate her child's need for reassurance; where possible, she tries to forestall anxieties.

The only way we can begin to understand what children endure, or relish—and so both help them through difficult times and enhance their joy—is to remember that we were once children ourselves, and try to remember how it felt. Children conceal things. "Not to expose your true feelings to an adult," Orwell writes, "seems to be instinctive from the age of seven or eight onwards."

In this book the stories of twenty-two adult children of older parents are unfolded. In setting out their recollections of their childhoods, and their feelings about them, no claim is made that these people speak for *all* "late" babies. From their words, though, common anxieties emerge. Analysis of the interview transcripts draws out differences and similarities between and among the memories, and separates out that which is unique to "late" children from that which is unique to an individual child, or from that which is common to all children, regardless of the age of their parents.

2

Feeling Different:
The Age Factor

She looked different from mothers of my friends . . . so much older . . . I was
embarrassed, ashamed . . . —Christine, born when her mother was forty-six

I remember being really repulsed by my Mom . . . her shape. She wasn't a
very physically attractive woman to me, compared to, like, the kids next
door's young Mom.—Barbara, born when her mother was forty.

Most children are conformists. They prefer not to be different
from their peers, not to stand out from the crowd. One season,
for instance, all the young girls iron their long hair and wear it
parted in the center, falling forward to frame their faces as
symmetrically as though arranged with a micrometer. Another
season, simultaneously it seems, they all begin sporting big,
luridly colored, plastic clips on the tops of their, now, wild and
curly heads.

Given this seeming need of youngsters to be like others,
how, if at all, are late-born children affected by being different
from most of their peers? How did those interviewed for this
study become aware of their parents' ages and how did they
feel about it?

With few exceptions, they remembered vividly the times their parents were mistaken for their grandparents, and the anguish that brought:

"I was *very* aware that they were older. How? Just by looking at them. I mean, it was easy to see. I went to a Catholic school with large Irish families and Mexican families and not only was I an only child, but the only child of older parents. And people would ask if those were my grandparents and I would *die* of embarrassment. I mean, when you're a child, you want to be like your peers and it's sort of hard to handle."

This, from Cheryl Greenham who, through her job as teacher in a private elementary school, has come to understand the needs of children. Cheryl was born when her mother was forty-three and her father was forty-eight years old.

"And I was really hard on my mother." she continued. "I mean, I was cruel. I could be extremely cruel. At one point, I actually asked her for my birth certificate . . . this was when I was eight or nine years old . . . 'Let me see,' I said. 'You're too old to have me. Let me see that I'm your natural child. You must have adopted me.' That must have been pretty hard to take."

"Has she forgiven you?" I asked her. We both laughed; Cheryl is now thirty years old.

"Oh yes. She was pretty mellow and pretty understanding. I guess she just took that as part of the territory. That she had this kid late in life and, like I said, I could be extremely cruel . . . I remember at fifteen being very angry with her and . . . I now regard it as unforgivable . . . I said to her 'Why didn't you just have another miscarriage!' " Cheryl had already told me of her mother's several unsuccessful attempts to carry a child to term. "*That* I was not forgiven for quite as easily . . . but, you see, I could be very angry and sardonic with her."

Cheryl remembers, too—and still regrets—that her father spent little time talking to her when she was a child. "He didn't know how to ... talk to a little girl ... and then ... when I was a young woman. After all, he was forty-eight when I was born. He didn't mean to be cruel. He just didn't know ... didn't understand.... He was so old ... But I had an uncle, much younger than Daddy, who I was really close to and looked to for those little wisdoms you get from Daddy but which my father didn't supply. I would go to him when I had problems or wanted to talk about something, because he would talk to me! And listen. I would feel comfortable with him. You look for whatever you need if you're a survivor. I wish Daddy had paid more attention to me." Her tone was wistful even though decades had passed since her early childhood.

Jean Smythe, born to a single mother of forty-three, remembers being especially aware of the social meaning of age, of her mother's age, particularly. "I might have been less preoccupied with it if she'd been comfortable about it. My mother lied to me about her age. And I found out. And I got the feeling it was something we couldn't talk about. I think if we could have talked about it, I might have been able to feel less anxious about it."

She and her mother didn't talk about her mother's age until Jean was thirteen when, in a burst of anger, her mother mentioned how old she was. "She thought is was a secret that was coming out of the closet and I was supposed to be shocked. In fact, I had known about it since I was five or six."

"Were you able to discuss it then?" I asked.

"No. After it was out of the closet, we didn't talk about it at all. We sort of had a conspiracy of mutual silence."

Sometimes Jean's mother was mistaken for her grandmother.

"That occurred a number of times," Jean said, "and if people made that mistake and were corrected, they felt a certain embarrassment and, usually, they'd try to repair the situation and become ... It was sort of like they put their foot in their mouths."

"Were *you* embarrassed?"

"Not embarrassed. Just saddened by the reminder."

"Were you saddened because your mother wasn't open about revealing her age to you?" I probed.

"There was something problematic that we couldn't talk about ... *that* caused me a lot of anxiety. It was the fact of her age *and* the fact that we couldn't talk about it. Both of these things saddened me, caused me anxiety."

An only child of a single parent, Jean remembers often being lonely. It was not enough, she says, that her mother was able to provide adequately for her material well-being.

"A kid doesn't give a damn about socio-economic status!" she insisted. "Childhood is universal and a poor child doesn't know he's poor and a rich child takes it for granted. I guess I was a rich kid and you bet I took it for granted! Sometimes I would go across the street—we lived in expensive apartments—to a much poorer house; they had four children and a young mother and a drunken young Daddy, and they played in the yard and the home always smelled of peepee and diapers, and they ate things my mother couldn't abide the thought of ... and I was over there all the time."

Charles Finch would have disagreed vehemently with Jean Smythe about the importance of socioeconomic status for children. For Charles, so proud of, and so loving toward, his older parents that he asked to tape our interview on his own recorder so he could later play it for his mother and father, his parents' middle-class income was crucial to his childhood contentment.

My concern that his answers to my questions would be so carefully phrased for his parents' ears that they would be a hymn of praise rather than a free outpouring of memories was quickly realized.° For the first hour, Charles offered his ap-

°Charles later decided not to play the tape for his parents. As happens with recorded interviews, he forgot the recorder was on and spoke of his dismay at the way his parents were aging, and the changes he must make in his life if he were to take care of them, and other misgivings that he would not want his parents to hear.

preciation of, and thanks to, his parents and to his older sister. We spoke on several other occasions, however, and his deep love for his family, and their love of him, were unwaveringly reiterated.

Charles was a much wanted child, born thirteen years after his sister into a well-established, upper middle-class family when his mother was thirty-eight and his father was forty-four years old. A baby-boom baby, born in 1946, several of his same-age friend also had older parents.

"I don't think age dawned on us until junior high school."

"And how did you feel then?"

"Well, I always felt rather lucky, because everyone loved my parents. So many friends and some relatives had told me they wished my parents were their parents, so it never occurred to me that their greater age was a drawback."

He has always felt that he owes his parents a lot.

"Did you feel under pressure to achieve, to aim high?" I asked.

"Well, I grew up in a very high-achieving community, so I would say the need to achieve stemmed from that context more than from any pressure from my parents. Sometimes I would get fifty cents for an Excellent grade, but it was never pushed at me, no. I just generally tended to do well." He paused, deep in thought, before continuing.

"There's an old Kennedy family phrase: 'From those to whom much is given, much is expected,' and I've been handed, not quite life on a silver platter, but I've been given enormous advantages. My parents could have done much more for themselves—traveled to Europe and things like that—that they didn't do. They sent me to the University of M., paying out-of-state tuition all the time... you feel a need to repay... for those sacrifices."

Charles is convinced that his parents' ability to give him so much was because they were mature and established by the time he was born, not struggling, as do many younger parents in the early years of their married lives.

"I'm all for people in their late thirties and forties having children. The chances are that somewhat older parents will have higher economic resources ... I get very angry when I see people who have no economic means having child after child after child because ... I was raised—probably being given *too* much, just about everything I wanted—and my parents were just marvelous people." He paused briefly, and then went on:

"I go to some fairly inexpensive places to eat once in a while, like Shakey's, and you see young parents dragging their kids in there ... And the parents in their twenties, still kids themselves, are still growing, and when they've got these kids, there's no question the children are something of a handicap. It's an enormous burden in this day and age when white middle-class people, particularly, are postponing childbearing because they simply can't afford it. They want to get a house, cars, and stuff like that. And when you're in your twenties ....God! When you don't even have a house yet, and houses cost ....Phew!

"*Some* people may say they don't care about material things, but I think we have plenty of evidence that kids are very aware of the social standing of their parents at a very early age, very aware when they can't have things. I think money and stuff like that does make a difference. And when parents are older, they're going to have a little bit more and be able to provide the kids with things. I know it's no substitute for love but, on the other hand, in my experience, my parents were able, as they said to rather enjoy me."

Unlike some others in the study, Charles felt no shame, embarrassment, or sadness in introducing his parents to other people.

"Whenever people met mother and father, they'd say 'What a wonderful lady and gentleman!' and there was one junior high teacher who actually expounded on what wonderful parents they were for about six minutes in front of the whole class. In a way, I was very pleased but in a way, you feel you have to live up to that. My parents were always there, always supported me, no matter what I did. I think, to some extent, when you're older, you're wiser, older and mellower."

"Did your parents ever punish you?" I asked. "If so, what kind of punishment did they use?"

"They rarely punished me. I was slapped a couple of times when I did or said something really horrible . . . but, I was a pretty good kid. On the other hand, my sister was a little more difficult to raise . . . so I think she was spanked more often. Then, again, they were younger then. With me . . . they were indulgent of me. It was just mutual love, back and forth. So I never did anything to hurt them."

"It sounds rather idyllic, I must say."

"Yes. It was."

"Your mother didn't go out to work when you were a kid. How much difference do you think that made to your pleasure in family and home and mother?"

"A great deal. I mean, people should be free to make the choices they want . . . but everybody seemed to be raised that way . . . had a full-time Mom. I loved having a full-time mother. I think people need that to a certain age . . . or either parent . . . .If I'd been plunked in a daycare center from age four or five . . . I dunno."

Unlike Charles Finch, Christine Strongman, whose mother was forty-six when she was born, was not proud of her mother.

"The first time I became aware of her age was, of course, when I went to grade school. She was so much older . . . she looked different from the other mothers . . . and I was embarrassed, ashamed to have her come to school and pick me up . . . I wouldn't introduce her to my friends if I could help it."

Peter Cochran, on the other hand, twenty-two years old and about to graduate from college, spoke at length of his delight in his older parents. He saw his happy childhood as directly due to the age of his parents, his mother thirty-nine and his father thirty-five years old when Peter was born.

His parents' age, he says, never embarrassed him. It hardly entered his consciousness until he reached his teens. "My parents, to this day, remain very young people to me." He and his parents formed a close grouping of three, sharing, it seems, all their home-based activities. For instance, as a child, Peter did not watch television alone; his parents selected programs and they all watched together. His friends with younger parents did not have his advantages, he said. "How many parents are going to drag 'round museums when you're a child, and keep pace, or set the pace for you in lots of activities?"

"Why do you think younger parents can't do that?" I asked him.

"Well, many of my friends with younger parents . . . their parents . . . weren't so involved with them." He hesitated, and then continued:

"Within our little family, we were always very active and we always had our own pursuits. It's only since I've been aware of families with very extended groups of kin that I questioned at all whether or not this [our family pattern] was good or whether or not I was satisfied with what I got out of it. The way I think as an individual is much different from the people who have had, who have, these extended filial relationships. I don't think it's bad. It's *different.*. My parents set examples for me that younger parents do not."

I asked Peter how his mother and father coped with his teenage years when they were well into their fifties.

"I was a calm teenager," he replied.

"Yes. But what about getting on your little old motor bike? Boys seem to go through that phase, while their parents sit at home with their knuckles in their mouths."

"I was sternly told that I would not have a motor bike. I could agree with that because I saw patients at the hospital where my mother taught, who had motorbikes—past tense. And I saw the condition they were in and I was made to know that was very likely to happen to me, so that was enforced. My parents wisely kept me active through my teen years with a variety of activities, swimming and skiing and so on, and they dissipated that teenage energy in fairly constructive ways. Wise move on their part! I never got involved in drugs or alcohol to the extent I see a lot of my peers doing. Maybe it was the example my parents set . . . . They set an example of propriety and calmness for me to follow."

"It sounds as though you were very lucky," I said.

"Well, a good comment on aging parents is that they do set that direction that many younger parents don't."

"Did you ever feel you were a little kid?" I asked. "The way you describe them, many of your activities were rather mature ones."

"No. I will say I was a little adult. And I sometimes find it difficult to deal with little kids. Yeh. I was considered to be mature at a very young age. I've taught swimming for a number of years and I do okay with very young children, but I have a real problem with kids about eight to fourteen. That's where I seem to have skipped."

"Those are the scattier years. of course."

"Well, I never went through that. Come to think of it, I've always had problems trying to figure out what was going on with people my own age. And I think that related directly back to the fact that their parents were so much younger than mine. A lot of things were simply not spoken about openly in our house; they were considered . . . private. I still feel that reserve, and my peers don't seem to. Their parents were . . . more open, perhaps."

During the course of our long interview-conversation, Peter gradually revealed that all had not been quite as perfect in his childhood as he wanted to believe, or wanted me to believe.

His parents were less than happy together, his father "ready to lump it fairly early," but they stayed together, Peter said, because they both wanted their child to grow up in a family. His mother, a perfectionist, serious about both her work and her play, unable to hold the marriage together and feeling herself a failure in this most important enterprise, turned to alcohol—("She's recovered from that, I think")—and the couple finally separated two years ago, when Peter was twenty years old.

Peter sees his mother frequently and was about to move back with, her, at least temporarily, after leaving college. He has less contact with his father. "We don't seem to be able to mend a rift that has developed over the last few years."

Jim Compton, now twenty, was born when his mother was forty and his father was forty-four years old. He is another of those, like Charles Finch and Peter Cochran, who appeared particularly eager to speak only positively of being the child of older parents. Even so, he soon expressed his regret that his father was much older than the fathers of the other boys at school.

"I just couldn't understand why he couldn't get out there and throw ball with me. I can understand it now, and I see what I missed . . . . And people used to say things like, 'Your grandpa's here to pick you up, or 'your grandma,' and they would laugh when they found out it was my parents. But I didn't think it was funny. I didn't like that; it seemed they were making fun of them."

"So you felt for them?" I asked.

"Right! Exactly! I didn't want people to think that they were old. It really didn't bother me," he assured me hastily, "but I wanted people to know they were wrong."

"When you were growing up—you're still growing up!—but when you were going through adolescence, those sometimes difficult years for kids, who did you talk to about your problems and the changes coming about in your life?"

"Well, mostly to friends. Friends and teachers. Or baseball coaches. I played baseball since I was small and I got close to a lot of coaches."

"Did you talk to your parents at all?"

"No. Not really. Because they had a different understanding than I think I wanted to hear. Because of the . . . era they came from . . . they had different thinking. But," he added quickly, "there's no really big area we disagree on. Just small things."

Like Charles Finch, Jim Compton sees older parents as being able to provide better for their children than younger parents might.

"I was never really deprived of anything," he said. "I think having older parents . . . they have more money saved. They have their life set. Whereas my friends' younger parents, you know, they were in and out of jobs to better themselves and they wouldn't have the money, say, to take good vacations like I had, or get a new bike . . . . It was a definite advantage having older parents."

Although both his parents worked outside the home—his mother as a hairdresser, his father in a bakery—they both returned home from work in the early afternoon and could devote time to the boy's school and sports activities.

"That's what I think was the best. My friends . . . their parents . . . well, when I played baseball, I think mine were the only parents who came to watch. They were always supportive of whatever I did. They'd go to open house . . . they were just involved with what I was doing. And though Dad didn't wrestle with me or anything physical like that, we played a lot of games at home, too, Scrabble and Monopoly and stuff. We still do."

Men, more often than the women interviewed, expressed regret at their parents', especially their fathers', inability to join in games with them. Donald Carter, whose father was forty-three when Donald was born, said, "As a boy, speaking of then, and your father is older and he can't get out and play ball with you and things like that. And you see kids your own age and their fathers are yet young enough that they can go out and play—you miss that. We both [my father and I] had an interest in sports and would spend time together watching it on television. It wasn't like being able to actually get out and participate."

Donald's awareness of his parents' ages, he said, in slight contradiction of his earlier remarks, "was never any kind of consideration in the household, within the family. But people outside the family brought it up. 'Is this your grandchild?' they'd say. And that made you feel kinda self-conscious about it. The only time I ever felt negative feelings about their age was when other people made comments about it. Left alone, and no input from outside the family, there was nothing but positive."

While Marilyn Henry, born when her mother was thirty-eight years old, appreciated that her older parents, by the time she was born, could afford to buy her what she wanted, she also regrets that they didn't do with her the kinds of things she would have enjoyed, such as camping, because they had already done them when they were younger and didn't have much money. When Marilyn was a child, she was taken on expensive trips, as was Jim Compton, but they weren't the kinds of vacations her friends with younger parents enjoyed and talked about—and that she wanted to talk about, too.

The need to be like the other children, to do what the others do, was also emphasized by Janet Spruce, age twenty-two, the middle child of a family of three adopted children. Her mother was forty, her father was forty-seven, when Janet joined the family as a tiny baby.

"With older parents ... they don't ... like, I had girl friends who always went camping with their parents ... and, well, my parents never ... well, when we were real little they took us, but since I really started remembering things—when I was about eight or nine years—they stopped ... I never went camping with them. And they'd never go out to the movies or out to eat. They just never got *out* .... I kinda missed that."

"Do you think it's because they were older," I asked. "Or not well? Or was is just their style?"

"I think it was because they were older ... because, my Mom, she's told me lots of things about when they were young. How they used to go out, whole groups, to movies and to dances ... It's like they got all their enjoyment *out*, like they got all that out of their system before they settled down to raise a family."

"So you didn't do the kinds of things you saw other children your age doing?" I asked.

"Yes, And that I would like to have done. My Mom was never keen on the idea of me doing things with other people, either. Visit my friends or go spend the night, or go camping with them. It was like, if we did that, she'd have to take *their* kids to do stuff."

"Did she go to PTA kinds of things?"

"Yes. She did that through elementary school and then that really stopped. She used to have my brother in boy scouts, but she never let my sister and me go in girl scouts, Bluebirds, or anything. She said it was just too much running around."

This, too, was a common theme running through the transcripts, the regret, the feeling of having been in some way deprived by their parents' inability or unwillingness to do the things that younger parents did. Barbara Anderson, at twenty-three, remembers becoming aware of her parents' ages when she was around twelve or thirteen. Her mother was forty, her father thirty-eight, when she was born.

"I was friends with one of the girls next door—and her family quite often would go to the JayCee picnic, or events at the Y, or play volleyball together. I always wondered why I had *never* gone anywhere, camping or anything, and it occurred to me, quite out of the blue one day, in our front room, looking across out the screen door to the house next door, that it was because my parents were so much older than their parents. And it kinda—I felt a little sort of abandoned by that. I felt I was being cheated out of a social life, or an eventful life. I sorta resented that fact." She went on, "They often talked about being too tired to do things, or they weren't feeling well. It wasn't expressed so much in terms of age but as 'I just don't have the energy to do this . . . . Why don't you go and do something by yourself or with your friends.' I remember thinking they were kind of an anomaly, an abnormal set of parents. They *used* to do things. They went camping with my older siblings. There are photos in the album of that. But not with me . . . . I think [my mother] thought she was going to have a last shot at motherhood and found she didn't have the energy for it."

Janet Spruce, among several others, does feel advantaged, though, by her parents economic stability.

"One thing I really did like when I was growing up . . . . My Mom and Dad, they waited longer to adopt us when they found out they couldn't have kids. And they had, like, some money saved up, which helped. My Mom never worked. She was always at home. Whenever we got sick—she still does it to me, brings me food in bed, you know, she's always there to help. And I used to listen to my friends in school talk about when they went home, you know. Their Moms worked and they had to go home, sick, and there wouldn't be anybody there. My Mom was always very sympathetic when we were sick, and she was always there for us."

Janet spoke of her awareness, when she was about to enter her teens, that her mother was menopausal.

"I remember her going through that. Boy, she was something else! You couldn't talk to her or anything, she'd snap at you so much. My Dad would tell us 'Oh, just ignore it. Just ignore it.' I wasn't really old enough to understand what was going on. We just kind of went around her all the time. But I can remember not being able to talk to her about anything because she was just having a bad time."

"At that age, you probably needed someone to talk to" I suggested.

"Well, I turned to my sister. We talked all the time. We were real close. Still are. She was the one . . . if I didn't have her, I don't know what I would have done. You need someone to talk to. And there was no way I could talk to my Mom. I still can't, to this day. It's a kind of gap between us. She doesn't understand my generation. She doesn't have an open mind . . . "

Priscilla Banks, unlike Marilyn Henry, Janet Spruce, and others, recalls the "differences" between her mother and the mothers of her friends with much humor and laughter. Priscilla, now a cheerful forty-year-old, remembers with affection growing up with her older parents:

"All the little girls used to dress up in their mothers' clothes, high-heeled shoes and all that. I went into the closet and I can remember thinking, I wouldn't want to wear *any* of these things! All my friends' mothers dressed so nicely . . . my mother's clothes were kind of matronly. She wore house-dresses and sensible shoes!"

Priscilla found the memory endearingly funny; others, though, still harbor profound reservations about the sizable age gap between themselves and their parents:

"When you wrote to me after my newspaper article was published," I said to Ted Martelli, the last-born child of Italian immigrants, his mother forty-two, his father fifty years old, when he was born, "you said that the fact of your parents' ages had a very deep effect on your life. What did you mean by that?"

"The first thing, I guess, is that I never knew my father as a young man . . . I mean, he'd had a number of jobs, for instance, done a number of things. When he first came over from Italy, some people from his village were icemen in this country; they sold ice. But after a while, he was an insurance salesman, then he took some classes in mechanics . . . but that was all long before I was born. Most of his life was lived before I was born . . . . That's what I mean about not having much knowledge of him as a young man. I know these things from hearing them from other people. What I remember was him retiring. But even when he was retired, he wasn't with me much. I do have certain regrets about my father not spending more time with me, although he had a lot of time on his hands. I guess it was just that . . . he was so distant in age from me so he couldn't have had much in common with me."

Ted doesn't remember his childhood as a particularly joyous time. His mother was often ill, his three sisters were ten, fourteen, and fifteen years older than he, leaving him feeling "isolated," and he had few people, if any, in whom he could confide. I asked him if he could remember any positive aspects of growing up with older parents. He pondered the question for some moments before answering:

"I don't know if this is really positive," he began. "I was thinking about the possibility that I didn't really perceive my parents as some people do, as people to rebel against, to react against, because they were really more grandfatherly and grandmotherly than motherly and fatherly. That is, people tend to love their grandparents and rebel against their parents. I think that's a common pattern, and that's because your grandparents are really not the prevailing generation. They are not of the generation of values that you are reacting against . . . and I think I had that sort of feeling for my father, for whom I had great love and admiration and against whom I really felt very little antagonism and rebellion. I think it may have something to do with the fact that he wasn't a young man who was any sort of threat to me . . . . As I say, I'm not sure if this is negative or positive."

Alice Marshall, now forty-seven years old, and one of those eager to tell me good things about being the child of older parents, also saw as negative the lack of ability to rebel.

"One thing I'm left wondering is, if my father hadn't died when I was fifteen and perhaps if my parents weren't these *older* parents, would I have experienced a more typical adolescent rebellion? That would have been important in my life."

"Why do you feel that?" I asked.

"Well, because I'm a student in the field, studying therapy, psychology, going for a license as a therapist, I think there was a time when all of us . . . we had anger that wasn't appropriately dealt with at the right time."

Although Alice was not emotionally devastated by her father's death, not having known him well nor having been as close to him as she was to her mother, she feels she was affected in other ways. Her older brother, for instance, had gone away to college and her expectation always was that she, too, would go away to school.

"When my father died, I felt my mother needed me and I felt some loss in that. Here it was, directly affecting my plans."

She went to a local college and lived at home. "I actually shared my mother's bed right after my father died . . . . I couldn't rebel, because I suddenly saw my mother as this poor elderly widow who had suffered this terrible, unexpected loss. She had never worked before and now, at nearly sixty, she went to work. She went to business school. We were suddenly in a difficult financial situation."

Like other late-born children, Alice was aware of her mother's age mainly because of the way she looked, compared to the mothers of her friends.

"She was gray—that was different—but I don't remember her behavior being different. All the mothers were housewives then, and mine did all the things that other mothers did, attended PTA meetings . . . . She was healthy, so I didn't ever think about her age. And when I started high school, I made friends with a girl who is still my dearest friend, and she was the only child of older parents. Her mother looked very much like my mother and that was reassuring, having that in common with my friend."

Alice had many friends but always one particular close girl, then woman, friend.

"Whether that was in place of my mother, a younger mother, I don't know. But I always had one friend with whom to be totally intimate, to tell all.... I *could* turn to my mother but... I don't think my mother knew very well how to deal with *feelings* .... I'd hold in a lot of feelings, not knowing if she'd know how to deal with me. She raised us to love each other and, you know, not to argue. She was a loving and nurturing woman but I never had the sense that we could work something through to resolution .... I remember more using my friends."

Alice feels fortunate in having had many friends, aunts and uncles, and a grandmother. She grew up, she feels, surrounded by people who cared about her.

Stephen Grey, in a quite different environment was a lonely and unhappy child, having few family members to rely upon, or to turn to, for comfort.

It never occurred to him that his mother was older than other children's mothers. He never even thought about it as a child or later. He attributes his miserable childhood to growing up without a father. His father, of whom he has no memory, died when the child was three years old.

His mother was thirty-eight when he was born and he can remember no play at all at home. His mother was a fast, voracious reader who spent most of her leisure time hidden behind the covers of books. After her husband's death, reading became her major escape.

Stephen carries a lingering and persistent resentment toward his mother who, he feels, should have perceived that he, as a child, found reading a struggle and should have done something to help him. He *could* read, he assured me, but not fluently enough to enjoy it, to lose himself in it, as did his mother.

He feels he received no guidance of any kind, except for the expectation, stated clearly and early by his mother, that he would follow in his father's profession and become a lawyer.

Charles sees his mother's age as immaterial and does not recall ever worrying that she might die and leave him, in the way his father left him. His resentment against her appears to stem primarily from her requirement that he be something he didn't want to be, could not be. As a child, Stephen felt neglected and alone. When he and his mother did communicate, she was guiding him towards what she wanted him to become.

"I didn't develop a complete identity," he said, sadly. "I was always very compliant . . . compliant with my mother's plans for my life."

Meg Perkins, now twenty-five years old, was aware that her parents especially her father, who was fifty-two when she was born, were older than her friends' parents. People would sometimes mistake her father for her grandfather but, she says, she hardly thought about it, "because he was real different, anyway, from what I'd seen of normal fathers. He was really his own person."

Meg's father had been in show business, traveling with musical groups, and was, Meg considered, full of fun and far more playful and youthful than the fathers of her friends.

"The age thing has never made a big difference to me. My father never seemed . . . When he was sixty-five [the age at which he died], he was not sixty-five as far as what people *think* a sixty-five-year-old should be. That's why I never really thought about it. And my mother—she's sixty-one now—stereotypically, she's not a sixty-one-year-old. I would say she's maybe a forty-five-year-old."

"Do you think you've kept her young?" I asked.

"Possibly . . . I've given her a few gray hairs." She burst into laughter. "But I think I have probably kept her young. Given her something to think about, anyway, something to worry about, to keep her feeling needed."

Margaret Pearce remembers feeling that her parents, both forty-two years old when she was born, were much older than everybody else's parents.

"Especially my mother. I felt very resentful. I can recall one time somebody—we were at a lunch counter, my mother and I—and some man next to me said 'You really should do what your grandmother wants you to do.' and I got furious! And I said 'This is my *mother!*' And I can remember getting extremely emotional about their ages when I was, I think, in high school. My parents had taken me somewhere and we were having dinner with a group of friends, parents and children, and the conversation ran to what we would do, where we'd all be, next year this time. And my father made a comment that, at his age, he didn't like to plan that far ahead. He wasn't *that* old, but I think he felt so much older than the other parents in the room that . . . I'd never heard him say anything like that. And I think that was partly what brought it out, just his sitting around and looking at the other parents. And I can remember getting extremely upset and emotional and in a very high-pitched voice saying things like 'O-o-o-o-h, n-o-o-o-o! You must never say . . . !' And he also got very upset and said, 'Now calm down. Just calm down.'"

Margaret felt she could not turn to her mother when she needed someone to talk to. Instead, she confided in her sister.

"And was that a comfort?" I asked.

"It was!" She was emphatic. "And I did turn to her a lot. A *lot!*"

Margaret, unlike Charles Finch and some other children of older parents, did not feel advantaged by her parents' greater affluence than that of her friends' younger parents.

"They were more comfortably off . . . consequently, when I was in my teens, my mother would shop with me. That became the one area where we communicated. She loved her clothes. And she would take me to those designer studios, the type of place you would go and sit down and some lady would bring you dresses from the back room. And I *hated* those clothes! I wanted my little corduroy jumper that you could buy in the town toggery."

"So, in a way, it made you different from the other kids?"

"Yes. It was *continuing* to make me different. Not only did I feel I had parents who were older and therefore I was different, but this was pointing out my differences. The clothes were not suitable. The lines were much too sophisticated for a thirteen- or fourteen-year-old girl. I mean, my body was the same size as a woman's, but the lines were wrong. It was just not a suitable thing to do."

"And you were probably a little bit too young to be able to say that clearly, as you are able to now."

"Yes. I couldn't. That's it exactly. But I felt it."

"Would it have upset you to have upset your mother?"

"No!" She laughed.

"Oh? You mean you would have told her if you'd had the words?"

"Right! That's right! We didn't communicate much. I didn't feel very close to her. I went to my sister when there were problems. And my mother was comfortable with that. She couldn't deal with the problems my generation . . . . Whereas my friends' parents seemed to go with the punches and flow, a little bit here, a little bit there. More flexible. They had an easier time with the times."

Sylvia Shaw, whose mother was thirty-eight, her father forty-one, when she was born, feels unaffected by her parents' ages and did not realize hers were older than other children's parents until she was in junior high school. She attended junior high with two of her cousins, whose mothers had been seventeen and twenty-three years old, respectively, when these particular children were born.

"It was *obvious* my mother was far older than my cousins' mothers. Her appearance told it clearly."

She does recall, when in the third grade, asking her mother

how old she was. Her mother promptly responded, "thirty-two" and Sylvia had no reason to question that. But when she was in the back seat of the car with some friends one day, being driven somewhere by her mother, one of her friends asked, "How old is your mother?" and Sylvia answered "thirty-two." She remembers her mother chuckling in the front seat, but she didn't understand why.

In retrospect, Sylvia sees both her parents as being "out of date" in their dress, in childrearing practices, and in other ways, but her two older sisters, ten and thirteen years older than she is, kept up with the latest fads and fashions, so she never felt deprived or in any way resentful.

She remembers some play at home when she was little. "My father used to give us horseback rides . . . but he stopped that when I was about six. He was then in his late forties, close to fifty years old. Maybe he was too tired."

One of my colleagues, whose academic specialty is deviant behavior, routinely requires his students to write a paper on some attribute of their own that they consider "stigmatizing."

Stigma were once bodily signs, discrediting symbols, signifying something morally bad or unusual about a person. The mark of Cain, or the A on the breast of the adultress Hester Prynne, alerted others that here was an evil person or, at the very least, one whose moral identity was tainted and who should be avoided or shunned. Now, the term "stigma" is applied more to the disgrace itself than to its bodily evidence. In his own mind, and in the mind of others who know about it, the whole person is diminished to his failing, shortcoming, or handicap.*

Knowing my interest in children of older parents, my colleague was eager to chat over lunch about a recent essay by one of his students. "People usually write about belonging to

*For the classic statements on stigma, see Erving Goffman, *Stigma: Notes on the Management of Spoiled Identity.*

some out-of-favor ethnic group," he began, "or having had a mastectomy. Or they tell of a crime they've committed, or of their addiction to drugs or drink, and the effect this physical or moral blemish has on the way they think about themselves and on their dealings with others. This man, though," he went on, "wrote of having older parents, parents far older than those of his schoolmates, and of his bitterness at being so stigmatized. He wrote 'I would never ask my friends to the house, I was so ashamed of my mother and father; I would never introduce my parents to anyone. As a child, I hid them, and I still hide them to some extent.' "

That a person would find older parents so discrediting, so shameful, that he would conceal them, as one might conceal from others that he made obscene phone calls or stole old ladies' purses for sport, surprised my colleague more than it surprised me. While none of the people I interviewed expressed such profound shame as did my colleague's student, many of them were ashamed of their parents' ages and appearance and felt themselves stigmatized by it.

Whether we like it or not, age is one of the characteristics by which human being assess each other. In our society, unlike some others, added years do not usually bring added esteem. We have few roles for older people to play, so we admire them if they continue with the same activities, in the same ways, as when they were younger. "He's wonderful *for his age!*" we say, or, "You'd never believe she's fifty! She looks thirty-eight, at the most!" On the other hand, "She's looking her age," is never meant as a compliment. Only when people are *really* old— when they have survived in good health into their eighties and nineties—do we allow them to feel pride in their years. Women, even more than men, are expected to remain "young" in appearance, dress, and manner, and multimillion-dollar industries rest on the premise that women, especially, will make superhuman efforts to retain their youthfulness. Susan Sontag, in "The Double Standard of Aging," published in 1972, wrote that this would change only if women refused to be parties to a convention that demeaned them and caused them anguish.

Many of those who are currently deferring childbearing and childrearing are likely to insist that *their* children will grow up in a different social climate from that experienced by past generations, even by those in the recent past. They feel that attitudes toward aging are changing as the population ages. After all, the median age in the United States when the first census was taken in 1790 was sixteen; in 1970, it was twenty-seven; it is now around thirty-three and is expected to reach forty early in the twenty-first century. With an aging population, it might be expected that middle-age and old age, as more common experiences would become accepted as distinct periods in life, not to be confused with youth, nor in competition with youth.

If Sontag's advice had been heeded, that might, indeed, be the case. Instead, the focus on youthfulness as the only really desirable state for all, men and women alike, has become sharper than ever, directed and encouraged, in part, by those who gain from the increasing emphasis on fitness and health, these terms often used synonymously. The youth and fitness industry includes the manufacturers of sports and exercise gear, cosmetics manufacturers, and makers of drugs and other products that supposedly retard the influences of the years. Sales of calcium supplements, for instance, have increased at least twelvefold, to around $240 million, in the past few years, in the wake of scare-tactic advertising that suggests that women will double over like hairpins if they do not supplement their intake of calcium as they age. This, despite scientific evidence that calcium supplements have little effect in slowing bone loss.

Signs of the anguish that accompanies aging are everywhere: on television situation comedies, in films, and in the press. On a recent installment of *L.A. Law,* Douglas, at forty-one, is the butt of much mirth because he is experimenting with hair-pieces. "Being bald is like wearing bifocals," he says. "You look like somebody's uncle. That's what you have to look forward to," he says to his thirty-seven-year-old colleague. "Take it from me," he adds, using hair loss as a metaphor for youth, "When it goes, it's gone!" A past lover's reassurances that it's more important to care about someone's "insides" than his appearance are less than persuasive when she introduces her new lover, whose "outside" is young, muscular, and topped by a full head of hair.

In the same show, an installment with aging as an important underlying theme, a woman accepts her lover's embraces with, "I hope by the time I'm forty, you'll be as happy with my face."

Perhaps the dividing line between youth and age is placed a little higher than it once was, especially for women. Perhaps it is forty, now, rather than thirty. "Forty is a threshold," Irene Goldenberg, a psychologist, remarked recently, in discussing Jack Benny's insistence on remaining thirty-nine for the last four decades of his life. "Staying thirty-nine represents a denial of the transition." Wendy Leopold, in the *Los Angeles Times*, cites heroic efforts, including plastic surgery, to remain young looking by those who are approaching forty. And a clinical psychologist credits the large numbers of those approaching forty for the quadrupling of liposuctions in the Los Angeles area. Other spokespeople, cited by Leopold, "equate forty with deep decrepitude."

More than ever before, *image* is of more importance in this culture than is substance. In our image-conscious society, gray hair and wrinkled skin are deplored and shameful. Many, perhaps most, are encouraged to feel they must erase these stigmata if they are to pass as "normal." The picture of the "perfect woman," for instance, reinforced constantly by media of all kinds, is youthful—and thin. This model of what women *should* be like has been shown to have profound effects on children: a recent study by researchers at the University of California, San Francisco, of 500 girls in grades 4 through 12 shows that 50 percent of the nine-year olds and 80 percent of the ten to eleven-year-olds surveyed said they diet to lose weight. The researcher concluded that these children's "fear of fat," even when they were not overweight, reflects "the culture's perfectionist attitude toward image." She spoke of a general—and frightening—intolerance towards any deviation in appearance.

Children soon learn the expectations associated with age, as they learn all the other norms of their society, and, as some of the comments and memories of the children of older parents indicate, they learn to feel shame and embarrassment when their parents are different from the way parents are "supposed to be"—when their parents are older than the parents of their peers. This is especially so if children are teased about their parents, if their parents are mistaken for their grandparents and disparaged as old, or if others' attitudes are perceived as disparaging, even if that is not the intention.

One family's way of attacking the age question head-on was described by Joyce Sunila in a recent *Reader's Digest* article. The father of a nine-year-old boy, forty years older than his son, had trained the boy to deflect any shame he might feel when asked if his father was his grandfather, onto the questioner.

"No," the child would respond. "He's my great-great grandfather. He's over ninety years old, and he rode his bike all the way here, four hundred miles, from New York City." According to the article, "The questioner fled in embarrassment," and the boy and his father laughed together later, when the child recounted the event.

Turning a potentially shaming incident into a game and a joke may work to reduce pain for the child but the article presents the story from the adults' viewpoint; we do not know how the child might be affected by this, perhaps extreme, retaliatory tactic.

Some children in this study, though, were not conscious of their parents' "difference" until their teens, if then. Mom was Mom. She was there. Like most of the other Moms, she was at home all the time, available after school with milk and freshly baked cookies. Mom was warmth, comfort, shelter. She was loving nurse when a child was sick.

Even those who felt ashamed of their parents' "older" appearance, of their being mistaken for grandparents, did not all regard it as of great seriousness or of lasting importance. Some, like Priscilla Banks, who said she had been a happy little girl, laughed heartily at her memories of her mother's frumpy, matronly clothes. Her deep affection for and closeness to her mother allows her to see her mother's "difference" from the other children's mothers as endearing, as something for which to love her mother *more*, rather than less.

Others, though, still cannot laugh when they remember their years of growing up with older parents. For them, the problems were not only of the *appearance* of age, they also stemmed from the physical changes that age brings and from the attitudinal distance between themselves and their parents.

Many people in their late thirties and early forties are enjoying the best time in their lives. They have developed opinions about the world based on experience, they know who they are and how they feel about important personal and social issues. For those in the middle and upper classes, careers have taken shape; solid achievements can be documented, allowing confidence in the attainment of other, higher goals. Life is good and the future promises progress from strength to greater strength. A good time, many now believe, to start a family and bring to that enterprise the experience and the financial security gained during the earlier, taxing years.

Children born to these more mature men and women, though, indicate that perhaps some of the energy, the zest, given to career building, to becoming established, or just to living is not necessarily renewable forever. For instance, even if a father feels himself at the peak of his abilities at forty when his son is born, he may simply feel a bit tired by the time that boy is in his teens. He may not have quite as much energy to play ball as he had ten or fifteen years before. And the mother in her fifties, entering or passing through menopause, may have less patience for the scattiness of a teen-age daughter than even the limited patience some thirty-five-year-old women can muster! This may be especially the case if that woman in her middle years is holding down a demanding, albeit rewarding, job.

Further, the thirty or forty-year-old who feels "hip" to today's world, or "groovy," and well in harmony with contemporary thought may, in carrying present attitudes into the future, be seen by his or her children as out-of-date and out-of-tune with the younger generation. Dora Sernat, a new mother at thirty-six, may speak for many women in their thirties and forties. She feels that social conditions have changed greatly, people of twenty-five and fifty now wearing the same kinds of clothes. This being so, she will, she says "keep growing younger" for her child. But one cannot will oneself to keep "socially" young indefinitely, nor predict how one will age physically. Much depends on genetic endowment—family history and family traits.

This is not to suggest that there is anything improper in being one's age or that a person must stay forever sixteen in heart, mind, and body to be a successful parent! The implications, rather, are that parents—older or otherwise—be realistic about what they can and cannot do for their children and be aware of their children's needs so they can help them meet those needs.

As few parents can provide everything for their children, just as few husbands or wives can provide every kind of satisfaction for their spouses, the task is to ensure that *someone*—an older child, a young aunt, a teacher—*someone* be available for the child, to serve as a surrogate parent, especially when, as is increasingly the case, both parents hold full-time jobs outside the home.

The least contented among the late-born children interviewed remember their childhood years as lonely; they had no one close to talk to. They felt they could not talk to their parents because the age gap was too great to bridge. Their parents didn't understand the younger generation, the children felt, or their parents were too far removed from youth to remember its anguish. At worst, the unhappiest children felt neglected.

It does appear that the ability of older, more established

parents to provide material things for their children is considered an advantage. Even so, bicycles or expensive holidays could not compensate for the lack of parental attention.

Some of the more contented children either had "full-time mothers" (always at home to minister to their needs) or parents who, even if they both worked, devoted time to the children's activities. The father who could no longer play catch with the boys was at all the games, with his wife, rooting for the team. Children appreciate their parents' attention, both at the time and in retrospect. It allows them to take for granted that their parents care for them and about them. It gives shape and stability to their lives. This holds, of course, whether parents are young or older, but for older parents it is even more important if the impact of negative social views about age is to be reduced.

3

Only Children of Older Parents

"Who did you talk to when you were a kid?"
"I'd talk to . . . a tree!"—
Stephen, an only child, born when his mother was thirty-eight

Only children are often considered at a disadvantage, compared to those who grow up with brothers and sisters. They are seen as missing the give-and-take of normal family life, the learning to share sometimes limited resources, including the time parents can spend with their offspring, the learning of social graces that comes with taking turns and participating with others in household chores. Only children are also often perceived as lonelier than children of larger families.

On the other hand, only children may be advantaged in some ways. They can command all the time their parents can spare from other pursuits. And any other childrearing resources—including money for college—will be available, intact, for the single child.

But what of the only child of older parents? Does he or she feel especially disadvantaged or, rather, especially compensated in some ways for the lack of siblings? And is the only child of a *single* older parent likely to be especially lonely?

Jean Smythe, a professor in the social sciences, is now thirty-seven years old. She was the only child of an unmarried mother who was forty-three years of age when Jean was born.

In the late 1940s, social attitudes toward single mothers were less accepting than at present but, when Jean's mother discovered her pregnancy, she was delighted, viewing it as some kind of "miracle." She had been told that she was sterile and so took no precautions to avoid conceiving.

A fiercely independent career woman, Jean's mother, much like some single women choosing motherhood now, was financially well able to care for herself and her infant. Further, her own mother, who lived with her, was happy to help with rearing the baby. Jean never met her father, nor does she know who he was. She believes he was a young man, much younger than her mother.

Jean was married at sixteen years of age, had her first baby when she was nineteen, and her second a few years later. She dismisses her marriage as "a farce" and says she was divorced "ages ago." For many years, she has lived with her lover, Bettina; Jean's teenage children live with the two women and understand their relationship.

At the time Jean was interviewed, her eighty-one-year old mother was in a stroke-induced coma in the hospital to which the parademics had taken her. She died a few weeks later, never having recovered consciousness.

Jean felt fortunate, she said, that her mother had lived so long.

"I began to think about death a lot when I was extremely young. In fact, at an age when, supposedly, children can't conceive of death. Very early in life, at about five, I could assess the probability of my mother dying and I realized there was a strong chance I might lose her when I was very young. I was always concerned about that, at an age when other children didn't seem to worry about it at all."

According to psychologists, pronounced fear of death, their own and their parents', does occur in some children at around eight years of age, but it is often provoked by an actual experience of death. Fear of death is generally rooted in fear of separation from parents, and one way to ease this fear for a child is to explain that death is for old people. But if a child's parents, or single parent, are already old, the fear of death may be difficult to overcome.

Her mother's forty-eight years seemed a very great age to the five-year-old Jean, who now speaks of her childhood "anxiety," her "obsession," and her "preoccupation" with age. Her early fear that her mother would die, Jean felt, had much to do with the small number of other social supports in her world.

"I had my grandma ... but I knew she was *really* old .... If there had been two parents ... siblings ... I remember often consciously thinking to myself it would be fine, if only I had some older siblings and ... sometimes I would ask, 'Mommy, are you sure you never had any babies before me? Are you sure you never did?' And I was always assured that no, she never had."

Jean can remember feeling a desperate need for a family:

"I decided that the only way I could have a family would be by making my own."

When she was barely into her teens, Jean became, she said, "obsessed with ways to promote fertility. I spent half my time in the gynecology section of the medical library, reading and reading, and the other half at the gynecologist's office. I deliberately tried to get pregnant and was frustrated when I did not. I must have been the youngest patient ever at the fertility clinic! All those older women, trying for years to conceive, and I ... in my teens!"

Jean was, she said, "terrified of being left alone. I prayed to grow my sister. She is, in fact, my daughter. But I grew her ... my infant sister." She speaks of her children as the brother and sister she never had.

Jean appears, too, to have known few other children before she went to school.

"Going to school was a huge shock to me. It was the first time

I'd met another child. My first day at school, I was crushed. For one thing, the children behaved so differently from people I had known until then. They pushed and shoved. I was brought up to be polite and stand back so that others could pass. And the teachers! At home, I was extravagently praised whenever I did something right. If my mother didn't approve of my behavior, she simply said *nothing*. So, when teachers didn't praise me, didn't make any remarks to me, I was sure I had done something wrong . . . and I didn't know what it was! My first day at school was crushing."

Unusually protected by her mother, and spared the hurly-burly, the pushing and shoving, that children take for granted when they grow up with brothers and sisters, Jean was ill-prepared for the world, even the relatively benign world of kindergarten and the first grade.

"It was a terrible shock to find out I was just an ordinary person. My mother idolized me and I didn't have the basis for a realistic self-conception until later."

Jean's childhood, she concedes, was unusual. Her mother had no interest in the kinds of activities, such as PTA meetings and programs, that other mothers consider they must take part in for their children's sake.

"My mother viewed mothers as not *her*! They were a different aggregate. None of her friends were mothers. They were the kinds of people that generally pooh-poohed motherhood and didn't like children; I was always being told that I was the only child they ever liked."

There was not, then, much physical children's play at home when Jean was a youngster but there was, she says, "joy and play and entertainment. In fact," she added, laughing, "joy and play and entertainment and having a good time was *the* theme of my mother's life!"

Jean expressed strong disapproval of women who choose to have children late in life.

"I don't understand these women. They're supposed to be educated women, women who are sensitive and human, women who read, who have abstract minds... and they're doing the most selfish thing."

Asked if she felt that way about her own mother, she said:

"No. I think my mother was impulsive and ignorant, mainly. And she remained that way. She was a bright, talented woman but she wasn't very philosophical."

And when asked if her disapproval of older mothers was because she was, herself, the child of such a mother, she replied:

"I think it has a lot to do with that fact. I don't know how a child of a younger mother might feel but I *do* know that, by all standards of maturity, adjustment, self-esteem, happiness, etcetera, my daughter is *so* far ahead of where I was ... "

Marilyn Henry, a health-program administrator now age thirty-eight, not only is an only child, born when her mother was thirty-eight and her father was thirty-seven, but she also waited until ten years into her marriage to have her own child, when she was thirty-two years old.

Her choice to postpone childbearing was deliberate, she said, predominantly because of her career but, she added, her ambivalence still apparent, "I didn't consciously want to follow in my mother's footsteps, repeat her choice ... but ... making major decisions is not easy for me." She plans no additons to her family.

Her mother died at seventy-six years old, less than a year before Marilyn gave her interview. Her father is still alive.

Like Jean Smythe, Marilyn is grateful that her mother lived as long as she did because, as a child she, too, worried that she would lose her parents:

"Between the fourth and the sixth grades, the possibility of my parents' death was on my mind a lot; I remember waking up at night and going to their room and checking to be sure they were still there."

Marilyn, though, fitted more closely the psychologists' observations of children who worry about death than did Jean

Smythe: she was already eleven or twelve years old and her concerns, she said, were predicated on a specific experience of death.

"Relations of ours were undertakers and we visited them in North Carolina. As an eleven-year-old, I had a tour of the mortuary—*all* the mortuary! I believe it was then I started to think about death."

Marilyn worries now about leaving her own small child. "I really felt I didn't want to be an older parent because . . . as an adult I can see . . . the chance of dying and leaving . . . the children . . . before they're ready."

She is saddened, too, by the realization that, with her mother's death, few people remain who share her memories, who shared her past: "Even if it's a brother or sister you hate . . . You know?"

Marilyn had been very close to her mother who, although she did not "play" with the child, helped her to make clothes for her dolls and, Marilyn said, "we always cooked together and spent a lot of after-school time together. She didn't go out to work."

When she was growing up, Marilyn recalls, everyone else's mother was younger than hers and they did different kinds of things with their children from those her parents did with her.

"I never verbalized it because I thought it would make my mother unhappy . . . but, when I was a kid, my schoolmates were doing things like going camping, all the things my parents did when they were young and had no money. I would have loved to camp but *my* vacations were *travel* vacations, expensive trips. My first camping trip was not until five years after I was married."

Cheryl Greenham, enjoying the summer break from her job as an elementary school teacher, was not quite ready for our arranged meeting in the apartment she has shared with her mother since her father died two years ago. While I waited for her to dress—"I've had a hard time getting up since the school year ended," she later said—her mother acted as hostess, seating me in the comfortable living room and bringing me a cool drink. Mrs. Greenham appeared older than her seventy-three years—not frail but, rather, bent. Her misshapenness, I learned, was the result of numerous surgical operations over many years.

Despite a history of ill health, Mrs. Greenham seemed to have retained a lively interest in the world and to have remained active and cheerful. We chatted across a range of topics until Cheryl, an attractive, dark-haired, dark-eyed, thirty-year-old came into the room and Mrs. Greenham left us. Like her mother, Cheryl spoke easily, quickly—sometimes gabbling—eager to answer questions and to volunteer information.

Her mother was forty-three and her father was forty-eight years old when Cheryl was born. The couple had married relatively late, some six years before Cheryl's birth. It was a second marriage for Mr. Greenham.

Cheryl's mother became pregnant soon after the marriage, but miscarried. She suffered three more miscarriages before accepting that she would go through life without children. She needed a "partial hysterectomy," her doctor told her but, because she had made plans for the summer, she begged for a little time. "Let's put it off until October." By then, and without realizing it, she was several months pregnant.

"The doctor said he'd never seen such delight on anyone's face! This time, she was much more careful, rested a lot, and was able to carry me full term . . . I was the tenacious seed."

Laughing frequently as she spoke, Cheryl told of living in her imagination a lot when she was small.

"Being an only child, I used to have little people I talked to besides myself. I really lived in my own little world. I *was* lonely. I had a lot of cousins and I had a friend who is a friend to this day . . . . When you don't have someone, you *find* someone." And although two maiden aunts stayed with the family at intervals, Cheryl remembers being alone for much of the time.

"We had a dog. And that was it. But," she rushed on, "I wasn't totally isolated. I would stay with this uncle and his family for two weeks and that aunty and her family for two weeks . . . so I had my dose of children . . . . And my mother always welcomed my friends . . . . I mean, that wasn't really a problem. But I was . . . I always wished I had brothers and sisters and that it was . . . it was more like my cousins' houses. That's why I liked to go there. I think my parents were wise, letting me spend so much time with my cousins . . . so I wasn't totally estranged from the family scene."

When asked about the time her parents spent with her, Cheryl hesitated before answering.

"You know—being older, as they were—they didn't . . . we didn't do a lot of kid stuff. I think my mother saw me more or less like a little princess to dress up. She had performed this miracle of having a child and she was just . . . proud. And my parents never went on vacations. Vacations for them meant going out of state to see my mother's aunts. But I always went on vacations with my girl friend and her family. We'd go to the beach . . . . My parents just didn't go to the shore."

"Did they take you out?" I asked.

"No. They didn't *do* that. I'd go out with my friends but, as far as . . . I don't remember my mother playing with me. She was always there to talk to me and take care of me and we'd go shopping together sometimes . . . .She did spend time with me. I mean, I had ballet lessons and did this and that. I think, some-how, if I'd had someone to share it with, it would have been different." she stopped, deep in thought.

"I remember," she continued, after a long pause, "when I was about four or five years old, being absolutely in love with my father . . . the typical, 'I want to marry you, Daddy, I love you so!' But . . . he used to bug me. I mean, after the initial loving him, I used to get very angry at him. Because he was not affectionate. He . . . just didn't talk to me! He didn't take me to baseball games. He didn't... and I didn't know how to ask for... those things. Of course, he was forty-eight years old when I was born."

"Fathers often dote on their daughters," I prompted.

"I know. He didn't dote on me but, well... the one gift he did give me was an electric shaver!" She laughed heartily. "A *used* electric shaver! It *is* funny." She could appreciate the joke now, although it was evident that she had not been amused at the time.

"I really wish my parents had done more things with me. I mean, I don't see myself as underprivileged or anything, but it would have been fun. And it would have been good for them... kept them young, you know, instead of staying in their... adult world. I missed that... attention. Especially from Daddy. I always wanted him to... just... talk to me more. My best friend, Katy, he always used to tell *her* how pretty she was. 'Oh, Katy's so beautiful!' and I would get so jealous! 'Why doesn't he say that to *me*? I'm pretty, too.' And I would get very hurt. I don't think he meant to be cruel. He just didn't know any better. I mean, my being a girl, a young woman, was so far removed from.... He didn't understand what it was to be a young woman. He was so old."

Cheryl, like Jean Smythe and Marilyn Henry recalls being terrified about her parents' mortality.

"I can remember, at one time, just *weeping* in my bed. you know, afraid that I would lose my parents and that I would be left alone. I was just shaken. I don't know what incident precipitated it but... I remember those deep feelings.... Sometimes I just didn't want to deal... with... things... and I'd close them out. Float off... I was a dreamer... almost catatonic, at times."

Few people speak of their childhood as a time of undiluted joy. Even those who were surrounded by loving, caring family members and whose parents provided them with all the material things they needed or desired, will usually recall some hurt, however small, some incident, perhaps, to mar their memories of an otherwise perfect childhood.

Peter Cochran, however, twenty-two years old and about to graduate from a highly regarded small, private college with a double major in biology and economics, was eager to assure me that his childhood had been perfect, ideal in every way. A serious young man, fair of coloring, and wearing glasses that underscored his scholarly, bookish manner, Peter spoke fast and easily, never at a loss for words.

His mother, whose first husband had died young, was thirty-nine, his father thirty-five, when Peter was born.

"I would not have wanted parents to be a great deal younger than mine because I revelled in both their experience and their patience," he said at the beginning of his interview, establishing immediately his approval of later parenting. "And I felt very satisfied by having older parents. I know it has greatly influenced me in my thinking about when to have children and how I would bring my children up. The opportunity to speak to you," he continued, a little ponderously, almost as though he were lecturing to a college class, "was one I certainly wanted to participate in."

His mother and father had both been in professions that absorbed them, his mother a coordinator of nursing education at a large hospital, his father in the merchant navy, but both parents devoted substantial time to their only child, time, Peter remembers, in which they were lavish with their attention.

"Who took care of you when you were little," I asked him, "if both parents were working outside the home?"

"For the first few years, my mother worked part-time. She took a year off immediately after her pregnancy to care for me. My father—the situation was a little unusual there—as a merchant marine, he spent large amounts of time at home *all* the time, and then he would be absent for a great deal of time. In those periods, we had a live-in housekeeper to take care of me. And, by the time I was in school . . . my mother's schedule coincided very closely with mine, so she'd generally be home about the time I would come home. Or my father would be home."

"So you didn't feel in any sense lonely?" I asked.

"I . . . er . . . In a way, an only child is always aware that he doesn't have brothers or sisters around to participate with and I think you tend to compensate with other pursuits."

"What would they be?"

"I . . . er . . . Reading, for me. Also I lived on a game preserve, so I used to run around and collect bugs and butterflies. Watch birds. And I also was, I should stress, very active with my parents. We would always . . . if they were doing something, I was always there, part of their activities. That meant, if they were to go out to a museum or to a restaurant, I would be invited to go along. I would contribute too. And if they were busy with their hobbies—gardening for my mother, model building for my father—I would participate in those as well."

He remembers his parents as youthful, energetic people whose activities were centered about their professions and their hobbies and he says he was not aware his parents were older than his contemporaries' parents until he was about eleven or twelve years old.

"And then, how did it . . . strike you?" I asked.

"It was sort of *odd*—I remember I was visiting a friend and her parents were out but her grandmother was there. And her grandmother was no older than my *mother*. I still think of my mother as my mother and I have a very difficult time associating people of her age with being grandmothers.

"And then I also got to realize that my parents seemed a lot more interested in what I was doing, and in my concerns, than many parents who were much younger. My parents were very involved with my upbringing. I see that as something one gains with age . . . that kind of patience to bring up a child. 'Cos it does take a great deal of patience. Most of my friends with younger parents didn't have a similar experience of their parents being involved with them, their parents taking them to cultural things, taking them hiking. My parents were very involved, and I see it partly as a function of their age. Age gave them the ability to define their interests and pursue them. In my parents' case, they chose *me* as their major interest as opposed to any number of social activities or professional activities they could have been involved in. My father articulated that he gave up trying for a higher position because of the demands it would have made on his time, time he would not have had to spend with me. I was always very aware that my parents were conscious of devoting time to my upbringing as opposed to other pursuits and I never got a negative sense from that. They always made it very positive. It was something they were glad to do."

Peter launched into several long monologues of similar sentiment during our several hours together, constantly reiterating his parents' devotion to him and to his upbringing.

"My parents did *not* use television as a babysitter. We had one and I would watch *with* them. They didn't really like me to watch television by myself. If there was something on they wanted to see, I was allowed to watch. It wasn't 'Go and watch tv now!' while they went off and did something else. If my mother was preparing a lecture, I would be reading or doing homework. If my father was working in the basement on one of his hobbies, I would be there with him. Or if they were cooking, I would be in the kitchen helping."

Reservations about his parents began to emerge when he spoke about his early adolescence.

"I could talk to my mother and father about sex—my mother had nursing training so, as far as the mechanics of sex went, I learned that early. It was . . . the problems of a teenage boy trying desperately to express himself as a sexual individual. Twelve and thirteen weren't wonderful years for me, in terms of how they handled that. I know it was a little difficult for them to deal with me acquiring a sexual identity and I think some of it was because they were a little out of touch with those feelings. Forty years is a long time! You tend to forget some of the details and some of the pain of that."

"Did you have friends and did you bring them home?" I asked.

"Yes. I had a much narrower group of friends than some of my peers but, yes, my parents encouraged me to have friends over. One thing . . . " He paused. "If there was a problem . . . " He paused, again, seeming to search for suitable words. "In many cases, *parents* end up being friends as well. There seems to be something that goes on between *parents* and I think my parents were isolated from that in a way, because they were substantially older than the parents of my friends. In many cases, ten or fifteen years, and there's a large difference in the way people behave and think."

"Would you have liked the parents of your friends to be friend with your parents?"

"Yes. I would have appreciated it. But I always sensed there wouldn't be the closeness I saw between certain sets of parents. My parents' interests weren't the same, they didn't have the kinds of peer relationships, age-cohort relationships, with them . . . . It never developed past mere acquaintance."

Peter's parents had few friends of their own age, either.

"My mother just didn't have the chance to cultivate friends. She was always very . . . *driven.*" Later, he added, "In driving herself, I think she may have neglected some of her own development. And that absolute demand of one's self is not a completely constructive thing. It's wonderful to mouth that you accept complete responsibility for yourself . . . but that demands so much from you . . . I really would have felt happier if maybe she'd . . . they'd . . . had a group of friends they could rely on a little bit more. The closeness of our little family was wonderful, and it was nurturing, but maybe *they* needed to take a little bit more for themselves. Everything my mother did: professional involvements, childrearing . . . were so important to her, weighed so heavily. She really needed something that didn't *matter* as much. That she could have just played at. Everything was extremely, extremely important to my parents."

As our dialogue—more often monologue—continued, Peter unfolded his career plans, immediate and long-term, listing the degrees he expected to attain, the field work he would experience, and the career steps he would climb, each by a given age.

Asked if he felt, or ever felt, under any pressure from his parents to do well, to perform, he replied,

"I'm not sure they articulated expectations for me to perform well. I think I created them for myself. I expected myself to be very capable and meet or exceed all of the goals I would set for myself—and, at times, I've asked absolutely outrageous things of myself—or that were implicit in my parents' actions."

"So it was by example rather than words?" I asked.

"Yes. Exactly. My mother more than met her professional and social commitments, and she provided the time and attention that I needed. I just hope that, in my genetic inheritance, I've acquired her stamina! I'm not always sure that I have, although I seem to be able to cultivate it. But she's extremely energetic and an extremely strong woman. I really do admire her. She's an *individual.*" He paused, then added, quickly, "I admire my father a great deal, too."

"Your parents' style of parenting seems to have worked for you because they spent so much time with you," I said. "You say they didn't pressure you but they set you a favorable pattern that you'd like to follow."

"Well, there are parts of it I find very rewarding. And there are parts of it I'm trying *not* to follow, although I'm very aware of catching myself weighing certain things very highly. Demanding a lot out of myself. Demanding a great deal of success, achievement . . . and I'm very aware that I'm starting to repeat the same thing that's gone before and knowing it's something I have to watch and temper if I am going to avoid . . . some of the problems my parents had . . . . They had some problems . . . not everything was completely positive . . . and the awareness of that is . . . good . . . . It makes for a more realistic assessment."

Peter spoke, then, of other role models, his professors, especially, many of whom had chosen to develop their careers before having children.

"I'll be thirty before I complete the major part of my formal education . . . and then what do I do? At thirty, I'll be trying to fight for a position on a faculty, publishing, giving it a lot of time. Will I have time to devote to children the way my parents devoted time to me? It'd be ten years before I'd be secure, which'd make me forty . . . and that's as old as my mother was when she had me. I think my childhood was a rewarding experience for me and I'd like to repeat it for my children . . . devote time, give them the opportunity to grow from my experience. I'd be more than willing to give it to them . . . . But what about career advancement, how much one wants to achieve? These are important questions."

"Do you think, then," I asked, "that your career will be so totally consuming that there would be no time left for the other side of yourself? For the emotional, sentimental, loving, giving side? It sounds as though you're considering denying yourself children until you've achieved this, that, and the other thing. Do you think it's impossible, then, to do both things simultaneously?"

"No, it's not. It's very difficult and requires a lot of energy and commitment, though. One is *never* established in one's career, I suppose. Even tenure is not the end. A person is always having to produce material, to be judged . . . . We still have the system to work within. If we want children and we want to succeed professionally, we really have to fight for it. I'd like not to have to plan every step . . . but, the way things are, one has to be very rational, very decisive, at every turn. Sad. Very sad. But," he concluded, returning to his earlier, more approving position, "I can't say that I'm not satisfied."

One only child of older parents who allowed no note of satisfaction to enter during his entire interview was Stephen Grey.

Stephen was born when his mother was thirty-eight, his father, thirty-five years old. A slightly built man, youthful, almost boyish, in appearance, he is, in sharp contrast to Peter Cochran, taciturn in speech. He appeared to think carefully before answering questions and rarely spoke at length, often punctuating, or ending, his statements with short, sometimes bitter, laughter. Single, he says he would like to marry and regrets his inability so far to find a compatible woman with whom to share his life.

Of more significance than the thirty-eight-year gap between himself and his mother, Stephen feels, was that his father died young, when the child was only three years old. Stephen has no memories of his father and feels a great void in his life. He grew up, an only child in a single parent family. His mother, a career-oriented professional, continued to work outside the home after the child was born, as do many contemporary working women; after her husband's unexpected and sudden death, she was able to support herself and her child adequately on her salary. She never remarried. A lively woman, now almost eighty years old and retired from work, she has a number of interests and retains a circle of friends and acquaintances gathered over the years.

"Do you feel yours was a lonely childhood?" I asked Stephen.

"Er . . . . Yeh!"

"What arrangements did your mother make for you when she was working?"

"Well, when I was very young, we had a colored lady . . . . Very nice."

"Someone who came to the home?"

"Yeh. She did the housework and looked after me. And when I got older, there wasn't anybody, really. I'd come home and no one would be there."

"So you were a latchkey kid?"

"Yeh."

"You'd come home, open the house, and wait for your mother to come home?" I probed.

"Yeh."

"Did you ever wish your mother was not working? Would that have made a difference?"

"Well . . . in retrospect it would. Yes."

"Do you think you were a happy child?"

"No." He laughed, a short, barklike laugh.

"And do you think that was entirely because you had no father?"

"Umm. Well, if I'd had a father, I might have been unhappy as well . . . " He was silent for a few moments. " . . . but I was guaranteed to be unhappy. Without a father. I just can't see any way around that."

"What do you feel about those women, then, who decide to have children without a husband? Often when they are in their late thirties, or even later. Do you think those children are going to feel the same as you did?"

"Well, yes. I do . . . but, on the other hand, I might do the same thing."

"Even though you see the children as being unhappy? What do you think would have worked against your unhappiness? What might have made for a happier childhood, given that you didn't have a father at home?"

"I don't think anything can take the place of a father. No one who comes in—a Big Brother—has the authority to fill that role. No, it just can't be done."

"So, are you saying that those women who are having babies without benefit of a husband at home ought to be aware that, for a child, there's no substitute for a father?"

"Well, yes, I guess so."

"When you were growing up," I asked, moving to another line of inquiry, "your mother and you must have spent a lot of time together, the time when she wasn't working. . . . Did you?"

"Er . . . no. I don't think so."

"So you didn't even have much time with your mother?"

"My mother is, always was, a very great reader. She reads very quickly and stays up half the night reading. So. It doesn't—didn't—really include me."

"Would you say there was any play in the house when you were growing up?"

"No."

"What was there for you?" I asked.

"Er . . . " He laughed again, his short bark.

"Did your mother read to *you* when you were little?"

"I don't think she read much to me, actually. I wasn't a good reader for a long time, which I find very . . . you know . . . er . . . disturbing."

"Do you read now?" I asked.

"Yeh. I'm a competent reader. But for someone who put so much stock in reading . . . she left it to school to do . . . yeh."

"Do you think that had anything to do with her being rather mature when you were born . . . ?" I began.

"No, That should have mitigated . . . "

"I mean," I said, "she might have been . . . settled in some ways. Perhaps it was a bit late to start including a child in her activities." I was probing.

"Well . . . No. I don't think so. I just think . . . in some areas . . . she has had some serious blind spots."

"It sounds as though you just don't feel you got much *parent ing* at all."

"That's right . . . Yeh."

"Didn't you feel yourself to be very important in your mother's life? I may be misunderstanding . . . "

"Yeh. I was important, but she didn't . . . I was very important to her and she went out of her way in a lot of areas to demonstrate that. But it wasn't in ways I would have liked"

"What might those have been?"

"Well, at first, I would like to have been taught to read properly, at an early age. And that might have been enough, or at least . . . "

"You seem to still feel a little resentment ... "

"Exactly!" He didn't wait for me to finish. "Yeh!"

"Have you ever spoken to your mother about this?"

"No ... She should have seen ... "

Stephen continued his brief, hesitant remarks, finding it difficult to express clearly the pain he still felt from his early years. He envied his mother her reading skill, her ability to escape into fabulous worlds, leaving him behind, lonely and frustrated.

"When you were worried, or troubled, as happens to all kids at times, who did you turn to? Who did you talk to?"

"I don't remember. I didn't ... "

"If you needed someone's shoulder to cry on?" I prompted.

"I'd talk to ... a tree!" Once more, he barked his short, dry laugh.

"That sounds rather sad. Wasn't there anyone you could go to, confide in? You bottled all this stuff up?"

"No. There was no one to ... there was no outlet for emotion."

"Do you think a brother or a sister would have done it for you?"

"Yes."

"But you could hardly expect your mother to have had another baby when you were born late ... and, in any case, she now had no husband. That wouldn't have been a solution."

"She could adopt one!" he responded, quickly this time. And then added, "I hoped this wasn't going to be terribly personal."

"Do you find these questions too painful?" I asked.

"Yeh."

Stephen's father had been a professional man, a lawyer. When I asked Stephen if he had ever felt pressured by his mother to succeed, he said she expected him, too, to become a lawyer.

"I'm not proud to say I went along with it, although I didn't particularly like . . . the subjects I had to take. But she said 'Go ahead and do it. And having done it, you can think about doing something else!'—that sort of thing."

After one year as a graduate student in law school, Stephen dropped out of the program and then spent several years working at menial jobs, searching for a different direction, one he would find pleasing. Only in recent years has he established himself in a profession, one rather more modest than the law.

In retrospect, Stephen said, he wished his mother had found another man to replace her husband. Profoundly lonely, he felt he had *no* parent, even though he had his mother. She worked all day, hid herself in her books for most of her free time, and the child was left, alone and lost.

His happiest times, if they can be so termed, were when he went away to camp in the summer. He liked the outdoors, especially looking after animals. He also found elementary school "very nice," he said, but even though he liked his teachers and had some friends, there was no one in whom he could confide.

"I think," he said, finally, "that the second half of my life is going to be a lot easier than the first half."

Rosemary Cross, a lively, witty woman of thirty-six, retains her delightful Scottish burr even after many years in the United States, first as a student and, later, as a program administrator. Her mother was thirty-five, her father, who had divorced his first wife, was thirty-nine when she was born, just nine months after her parents' marriage.

Rosemary's father, a career military officer, was away from home, often abroad, for long periods. At times, Rosemary and her mother joined him, as, for instance, on a two-year tour of duty in Tanganyika when Rosemary was between five and seven years old. At age seven, she returned to Scotland, where she lived with her mother and, for a time, with her mother's parents. Later, after her grandfather's death, she said, "It was just my grandmother, my mother and myself."

As a child, Rosemary was encouraged to achieve, to do well in school, but she did not feel pressured.

"It wasn't only my mother. My grandfather . . . would sit with his stopwatch making me go through my multiplication tables. It was *that* kind of pressure. And they'd always say 'If you don't do well, we'll still love you . . . . We'll just have to figure out something else for you to do.' But the automatic assumption was 'You will go to university.' The only real question was 'What do you want to do while *there?*' "

Rosemary had few regrets about her childhood years with older parents but she does see herself as having been "a rather isolated child."

"I think that had something to do with my father being gone a lot . . . and, because of that, my mother placed more emphasis on my being around her. I remember in my early years, really up to thirteen or fourteen, that my grandmother, my mother, and I spent most of our time together. So I wasn't off with my little friends. People who knew me back then say 'You were always old for your age!' "

"Was that because you were always with older people?" I asked.

"Yes! So I learned older people things."

"Do you feel you didn't have a chance to be a little kid? What kinds of games did you play?"

"I feel I didn't have a chance to be a *running-around* little kid. I was a sort of instant adult. I read a lot—a real bookworm. And I did a lot of jigsaw puzzles. Solitary kinds of things. Even when I went to school, it was home-based. It was literally over the fence from the house I lived in. So I didn't spend a lot of time walking to and from school." She paused.

"I think an only child tends to grow up very fast," she continued. "You tend to skip the silly stages of childhood. I was expected to be an adult. I don't think it's particularly good but I think it's something that older parents, especially, have a tendency to do. I have no recollection of being a silly little kid. And I really don't care for children now. Maybe I loathe them because I was never one myself!"

Rosemary felt the gap in years between herself and her mother more keenly as she entered her teens and her young womanhood. Although she was expected to be a "little adult" as a child, her mother was not eager for her to cross the line between childhood and real adulthood. It was not until several years after her contemporaries that Rosemary was allowed to discard her hated long knee socks for nylons, or that she could wear make-up.

Her mother's own style of dressing was staid, matronly—not glamorous.

"I really had no role model. My mother dressed solidly, sensibly, as she saw befitting a woman of her age and station. I couldn't say, 'She's not that much older than I am; I want to be like her.' It was not what I wanted to copy."

Meg Perkins, a pretty young woman twenty-five years old, with large brown eyes in a heart-shaped face and long brown hair curling about her shoulders, still watches her weight carefully. She was once, she said, very much overweight and she attributes that to shock at the death of her father, when she was thirteen and he was sixty-five years old.

Meg was born when her mother was thirty-six and her father, who had been married before, was fifty-two.

For Meg, as for Stephen Grey, her father's death was, she feels, the most significant event of her young life. Unlike Stephen Grey, though, Meg knew her father, adored him, and felt herself adored by him. His death left her shattered.

"I gained a lot of weight. And I started cutting classes. I didn't get into trouble with drugs or that type of thing . . . but I became very solitary. Very depressed . . . a hermit, basically. I'd go in and listen to a stereo in my room and be, like, *real* apathetic about everything."

Her depression lasted for about four years.

"Did you feel you could talk to your mother if you needed to?" I asked.

"Er . . . Y--e--e--s. And No. About some things. But she tended to be . . . a little bit overprotective, which I can understand perfectly now." She laughed. "The fact was, it was very frustrating and it usually blew up into an argument. So I tended not to talk to her."

Meg remembers the years before her father's death as "fairly happy." "I wouldn't say I was ecstatic as a kid." She laughed, again, "But I guess I was fairly happy. As a child," she continued, "I was pretty much a loner. The street where we lived didn't have any kids on it so I never really was out with kids. I was more into my own things. Drawing, reading, solitary types of games and things." Later, she added, "I think really the main thing I missed was having either a brother or a sister . . . and more kids around the neighborhood that I could go and play with." She did find company and comfort with an older couple she befriended who lived nearby. "They doted on me," she said.

Both her parents were musicians, her father a pianist, singer, voice teacher, and choirmaster, her mother a singer who also worked in advertising.

She did not feel pressured to achieve, she said, but "They *did* have very high expectations of me, especially my Dad . . . so it was piano lessons at five, and it was singing, which he loved, anyway."

Her parents did not participate in PTA or other school activities.

"I do remember thinking about that . . . that they weren't super-involved in that. They really didn't have time. My Mom worked full time, even then, and Dad was teaching all the time."

Asked if she shared activities with her parents, Meg said, "Well, we went on trips occasionally. My Dad usually played golf on Saturdays . . . but, yes, on Sundays we would all go to church where Dad was choirmaster. That was the thing we really did together. We spent most of Sunday together. I remember a few Saturdays, when my Mom and I would go to the movies or something like that. We were real close, but we didn't do a lot . . . we didn't go to places together. We had our routines and we were very close."

Meg's mother had stayed home for two years after her baby was born. After that, Meg went to nursery school; her mother picked her up after work in the late afternoon. That after-work time together Meg feels was important to them both. When she started kindergarten, she spent her afternoons with her father at home or, if he was teaching outside the home, he would take her with him. Later, as she moved through grade school, she would often come home to an empty house.

"I don't remember minding that. I was used to it. I would listen to records and play . . . and I would go to friends' houses, so it wasn't like I never played with anybody."

She had one or two close friends. Her parents, too, had a circle of friends, many from the church where they both sang.

She was aware early that her father was older than most fathers of children her own age.

"I remember one time when we were in a parking lot in a supermarket. He had me on his shoulders—I must have been six or seven—and some . . . man came up and asked me, 'Are you having fun with your grandfather?' " Meg laughed heartily, amused at the recollection. "That sort of made me realize that things were a little bit different."

But she never thought of her father as unusually old, compared to her friends' fathers.

"My Dad, he was very youthful! And playful. A practical joker. He never acted . . . older. He was fun!"

Meg feels strongly the importance to a child of being the "main thing" to its parents.

"Do you think you were the 'main thing' for your parents?" I asked.

"Er . . . Yes."

"You were really the center of their lives, do you think?"

"Oh, yes."

"You felt secure?"

"Yes."

"Do you remember having any worries when you were a kid, or any problems, doubts, concerns . . . ?"

She thought for several moments. "Probably self-confidence . . . . I think it had a lot to do with my Dad having . . . you know, living up to his expectations of me. What I should be doing. What I should be able to do. Being a Wonder Kid for my Dad."

"Did you feel you couldn't measure up? Is that what it was?"

"Not necessarily. I just remember being worried about it." She laughed. "You know, am I . . . enough? My Dad idolized me most of the time."

"So you just wanted to please him?"

"Well, I had doubts about whether what he kept telling me I was was *what* I was."

"Do you still have doubts?"

"Yes. I do."

Meg and her mother are closer now that Meg has grown up and, paradoxically, now that she lives in her own apartment, separate from her mother. Meg also feels an affinity with her mother's two sisters, especially the younger one, who had spent much time with her when she was growing up.

"They're really neat!" she said, enthusiastically. But, like Rosemary Cross she was among adults far more than with children. "People always said, 'She's so grown up for her age!' I never really felt as though I was a little kid. I was treated as a mature adult."

Contrary to popular myths, recent literature on only children indicates that such children are not unduly deprived. They are likely to have more possessions, although, say Sharryl Hawke and David Knox, in *One Child by Choice*, whether this is detrimental or beneficial may depend on how the possessions are given: to buy affection or, simply, to give the child an edge throughout life. The extra attention an only child may get from its parents can, again, be beneficial, but it can be detrimental if it heaps demands upon the child. Only children, according to Hawke and Knox's study, do appear very much aware of their lack of siblings and are also likely to be more "adult-like" than children from larger families.

In her book, *The Joy of the Only Child* (the title of which indicates its bias), Ellen Peck goes to some lengths to demonstrate the *superiority* of only children who, according to her study, were overrepresented as adults in many fields of endeavor, including arts and letters, social reforms, and sports. Peck does, though, admit to some drawbacks. "When there is an only child, the lens of the parental microscope—the focus of parental ambition—can overwhelm." Parental overinvolvement can be exacerbated, she suggests, when there is not only an only child but also a single parent.

H. Theodore Groat and his fellow researchers also found a few significant differences in adulthood between only children and children from two-child families. Comparing several thousands of subjects revealed that only children may be more cultivated and mature but less sociable; they may have had a less intense social life. Only children may be more academically oriented, but have spent more time in solitary pursuits and may be more likely to be "loners."

The stories told here by only children of older parents provide an indication, sometimes a strong indication, of the loneliness some such children feel during their childhood years.

A person can, of course, feel lonely in the middle of a crowd. Children in large families sometimes feel lonely or neglected but, as Stephen Grey pointed out, loneliness and unhappiness are almost *guaranteed* under some circumstances.

The chances for loneliness, according to the literature, are greater for an only child than for a child with siblings. And the only child who grows up in a one-parent home seems especially likely to be lonely. Further, when the distance in age between the child and its parent or parents is especially great, so that the parents have lost touch with the feelings the child may be experiencing, that child's loneliness is virtually assured.

Yet, not all the stories here tell of extreme loneliness. Jean Smythe felt particularly alone, and she was so terrified that her mother might die and leave her completely alone, she wanted—and tried—to produce "brothers and sisters" for herself as soon as she could. And Stephen Grey was a miserably unhappy child who, even at forty years of age, still feels the pain of his lonely childhood, still carries resentments he cannot easily discuss or dismiss. That both Jean Smythe and Stephen Grey grew up without their fathers is not to suggest that the late-born only child who grows up in a one-parent household will necessarily be lonely and miserable; rather, that a single parent may have to be especially atuned to his or her child's needs for attention and reassurance.

The others: Marilyn Henry, Cheryl Greenham, Peter Cochran, Rosemary Cross, and Meg Perkins, felt some loneliness; all regret, to varying degrees, their lack of brothers and sisters. But, as well as having their "solitary pursuits," most found, or were provided with, some substitutes for siblings.

Cheryl Greenham's mother encouraged Cheryl to spend time with her many cousins of her own age. "When you don't have someone, you *find* someone," Cheryl said. Not all the now adult only children of older parents were able to "find someone." They needed some help, some pointing of the way. Meg Perkins had aunts, some friends, and some grandparent substitutes to alleviate her loneliness.

I asked Rosemary Cross, who appeared to have been unaffected by, even unaware of, her parents' ages when she was growing up, why she felt she had been a normally happy child while others, in similar circumstances were, if not *un*happy, not truly happy, either.

"I think part of it was my unusual childhood. If I'd been in one place, all the time, with lots of little friends with mothers appreciably younger than mine, I would have noticed. But I think going from Scotland to Tanganyika, where the white colony was a motley crew, I had no chance to notice that 'all

these mothers are younger and here's my mother who is older.'
I was distracted, moving around.

"Also, my grandparents. They were sort of surrogate parents.
And, of course, they were even older than my mother, so I
didn't notice that my mother was older because here were my
grandparents who were *proof* that she wasn't old!"

Peter Cochran's primary companions were his mother and
father. Despite Peter's early insistence that his parents' attention to him, to the exclusion of all other interests except their
professions, was all that he could have wanted, some reservations about his "close family" gradually emerged. While appreciative of his parents' devotion to him, Peter is aware that
their close—perhaps *too* close—attentions may have been confining in some ways, and may have instilled in him his driving
ambition for professional success, a characteristic he sees as
less than healthy, either for himself or for his mother. Further,
as he, and his parents, grow older, he feels a measure of responsibility, even guilt, that his parents, especially his mother, do
not have the circle of friends they may need to sustain them as
he moves further away from the tight little family unit.

Children seem to need a variety of supports, besides parents,
when they are growing up. Even though siblings may often be
quarrelsome nuisances, they share one's history, they accom-
pany a person through the good times and the bad. Grandparents, too, can provide unquestioning love, as well as serve as
a buffer between a child's parents and *their* mortality. And for
the only child of older parents, substitute siblings—friends of
similar age—may help a child to *be* a child rather than a
"little adult."

Spending so much more time with adults than with children
may deny a child his or her time for normal childlike behavior.
Cheryl Greenham, Rosemary Cross, and Meg Perkins all spoke
of being "old for their age" or "little adults," and of never having really been children. Murray Kappleman, in *Raising the
Only Child,* suggests parents might include another youngster

at some meals, have the child invite a friend to dinner once or twice a week, and try to plan visits with other families with children of a compatible age. This would serve not only to provide companionship for the only child but also, by allowing the parents to see other children in ordinary situations, remind them what "normal childlike behavior" looks like. Participation in a child's school activities, too, while time-consuming and tiresome for many parents, might help provide him or her with a wider circle of friends and substitute parents. Jean Smythe's mother wanted no part in the PTA, nor was she interested in meeting other parents. And Peter Cochran suggested that his parents were isolated from the younger parents of his friends. Their interests were different. Stephen Grey's mother withdrew into the world of fiction when her workday was over, and Meg Perkins' parents, too, did not participate in school activities although they did develop a circle of friends through their church.

Some contemporary parents who delay childrearing until they are established in their careers are aware that the only child, especially of parents who are occupied, even preoccupied, with interesting work, or with each other, needs companionship. Dora Sernat, whose teenage children from a previous marriage live with their father, recognizes that the son born of her new romance when she was thirty-five years old is, virtually, an "only" child. She and her husband plan to provide a brother or sister for the little boy.

"It does seem rather unfair to the baby," she began. "Robert [her husband] and I are so wrapped up in each other, we feel the baby would benefit by having someone close to his own age because . . . I'm not sure we can . . . it's so hard for us *not* to be wrapped up in each other."

And Paula Parrish, vice-principal of an elementary school, also plans to increase her family soon—"We can't wait long for another child." Her first baby was born when she was thirty-six years old.

"We were not interested in having children or living as a

family unit until our mid-thirties—even then, my husband had to be persuaded."

Now that Paula and her husband have this first child, they see that the only child not only may be lonelier than a child with siblings, but that the only child also places more burdens on the parents than they can reasonably be expected to bear.

"Children who have siblings," Paula reasoned, "grow up in a more balanced situation—more balanced for the parents as well as for the children."

Many older parents of a late-born baby, though, may not want, or be able, to increase the size of their families. For the only child, substitute siblings, grandparents or substitute grandparents, inclusion in other families' activities, a circle of friends, and parents who devote time (but perhaps not *all* their time) to their offspring, may make for a more contented and secure childhood.

4

The Two-Generation Family

"May you live to see your grandchildren married"

"There's an old Jewish proverb, a blessing," said Ted Martelli—not Jewish but of Italian Catholic heritage—"and it embodies a traditional notion of a full life: 'May you live to see your grandchildren married.' To raise children and then see the grandchildren grow up and marry . . . I mean, you can't really ask for too much more than that, given the limitations of the life span."

Over and over again, as now-adult children of older parents pondered aloud about their lives, their early years and the childhood years of their own offspring, they expressed a feeling of loss, loss of generational continuity. They spoke yearningly of grandmas and grandpas either never known, or known only fleetingly, and of that same sweetness denied to their children.

"Did your parents know your children at all?" I asked Ted, knowing that his mother was forty-two, his father was fifty years old, when he was born.

"No. Unfortunately, they didn't. And that's one of the really great regrets of my life. My father died the year my son Tommy was born, the very same year. In fact, Tommy, who was named for my father, was born almost nine months to the day after my father died. And my mother died the following year. We were living out of state then and she never saw the baby."

"Did you know your own grandparents?"

"No. They all died before I was born. My own father was more a grandfather than a father, really. He retired when I was thirteen or fourteen and I never really did anything with him or went places with him. I always had very warm feelings toward my father, though, good feelings toward him. It's only that we were . . . two generations apart."

Ted Martelli's regret about the double generation gap between himself and his parents also sounded a theme often repeated in these interviews. Despite his marrying relatively young and starting a family quickly, his children, like Ted himself, were members of a two-generation family.

Jim Compton, whose father was forty-four when Jim was born twenty years ago was, like Ted, "kinda worried" when his father retired while Jim was still in high school.

"I was the only one whose father was retired, and . . . you know, you retire and that's the end of your life, really," Jim said, adding "and most of my friends' fathers were really involved in their work, starting new jobs . . . something like that."

Jim's father's parents died within hours of each other when Jim was about six years old. And his mother's parents, too, died so long ago, Jim hardly remembers them.

Frank Martin's father, in his late sixties, often speaks of retirement, although he continues to work in his own small business. Frank, at seventeen, finds he has little in common with his father, or with his mother. "It's a very difficult problem . . . because of the significant age difference between us, I find it hard to talk to them. When they're already old, they don't really understand what I'm going through . . . and when they're approaching retirement, what *can* you talk about?"

Meg Perkins' father, who had been previously married and who was fifty-two when Meg was born, died when Meg was thirteen years old. Meg was also very young when her grandparents died. "I vaguely remember my mother's mother, who died on Mothers' Day—a real blow to my mother—when I was . . . probably . . . four years old." But, although she had no grandparents of her own, she "adopted" an old couple, a device used by more than one late-born child in this study:
"They were grandparent *figures*, even though they weren't blood relatives. They lived in the garage apartment across from our yard and both spent a lot of time with me. They were doting, older type people . . . surrogate grandparents, really."

Donald Carter, another late-born child of a second marriage, born when his mother was forty, knew only one of his grandparents, and only briefly. "My two grandmothers died the year I was born, my mother's father had died years before that, and the remaining grandfather died when I was about five years old." An otherwise happy child, he regretted never having known grandparents. "I think there's something special about a grandchild and grandparents. Living here in Arkansas, family is important. You see a lot of grandparents, parents, and children interacting. And that's something I never had and I kinda missed it."

Jean Smythe, only child of a single mother of forty-three, was interviewed when her mother, age eighty-one, was lying comatose in hospital after suffering a stroke. Her mother lingered for a few weeks but died without recovering consciousness. Because Jean gave birth to her own children while she was very young, and because she comes from unusually long-lived stock, her children had known their grandmother until they were in their teens, but would not have her there to see them marry. Jean's own grandmother lived to see Jean marry and to see Jean's children enter the world before she left it at age ninety-three. But at only thirty-seven, Jean would soon become the "Omega generation"—the oldest person in her small family, the one with no generational buffer between herself and death. Not for her, pictures in the family album showing—as many albums do in those families where childrearing was started early, generation after generation—three, four, even five generations alive at the same time. In such a picture, Jean might still be two steps away from the Omega generation.

"That's something that's going through my mind now," Jean said, with sadness, "We're going to be a two-generation family . . . and I sort of want to be a grandmother now . . . but I don't know."

Stephen Grey lost his father so early in his childhood that he cannot remember him; he had few grandparents he could remember, either.

"There was only my father's mother . . . whom I didn't enjoy, really . . . I didn't look forward to my visits with her. Every six months or so my mother forced me to go over there. She'd keep bursting into tears about my father's death."

Among Stephen's greatest regrets is having no males, no father or grandfathers, as models. " 'Big Brothers' are not the same," he said, speaking of the volunteers who serve as surrogates to fatherless boys. "You need someone in your own family."

Even Peter Cochran, one of those interviewed who saw having older parents as a distinct advantage over being born to a young mother and father, had some reservations about the two-generation family.

"I'd love to be able to say that my mother will see me married and have children, but she might miss that. I regret the possibility that she might not see that."

Peter, although only twenty-two, is like several others in the sample: he has no living grandparents. Nor does Janet Spruce, at twenty-two, whose feeling of responsibility toward her parents grows greater with each passing year.

"I do feel concerned and I kind of do have a resentment, now that I'm older. It's like most of the kids *my* age, their parents are, maybe, in their late forties and early fifties .... It's like they shouldn't be that old, you know—my Dad's nearly seventy—and I don't want them to die .... You don't expect your parents to die until you've got a family going ... and some of my uncles and aunts even have grandchildren! On both my Mom's and my Dad's side, there are older brothers and sisters of seventy-five, around there, and they have kids who have kids that are around my age. And there's a person in *between* there."

Again, the double-generation gap is noted. And regretted.

And in speaking of having no grandparents, Janet Spruce said, "That's another thing that was really kind of sad. I had a grandmother on my Dad's side and she died in 1972 when she was ninety-some years old [and Janet was ten]. She lived in Oklahoma and I can remember seeing her four or five times. And I always remember the last time, when she was in the rest home. She was kind of senile—it was so sad to see .... I never had any grandparents. And that was weird, growing up with that. Everyone else had grandparents and I didn't have any. One time, there was this older lady who lived next door to us. We asked her if she could be our grandmother and she said we could call her that." Another "adopted" grandparent.

Her voice was strained as she continued, her throat constricting in her attempts not to cry. "I find it very hard .... There'll be no one there. If I have kids, I would like to have them in my late twenties, maybe early thirties. I don't feel ready for that responsibility right now. I don't want to rush it. But I wouldn't wait too long. It's just that there's a gap . . . and they won't have their grandparents. I'd kinda like to see grandchildren, myself, and I'd like them to see me."

And Margaret Pearce's parents, both of whom are now eighty-two years old, the mother with Alzheimer's disease ("sometimes she doesn't even know who I am") and the father who is in "precarious health," can have only the most tenuous relationship with Margaret's two sons, aged thirteen and eight years.

"For the past ten years, my parents haven't been able to do things. You know, I see all my friends leave their kids with their parents when they go off on a trip, or have their parents go on a trip with them . . . . My older son has a closer relationship with his grandparents because they were that much younger when he was young, and he was able to do things with them. My younger son, although he would love to know them better, he really can't."

Barbara Anderson's grandparents had all died before she was born and, for her, this was one more reason to regret being a late-born child. "I've again felt like I've missed out. Again, grandparents played a large role in most of my friends' social lives. They came for birthdays, and they were the ones that sent the best presents! And I really felt like, gee, I really didn't have anyone supportive. Because of that."

Marilyn Henry, still mourning the recent loss of her mother, was not only sad but also angry that her small daughter would be without her beloved grandmother.

"One thing I think about a lot is that when my father dies there will be *no one else*—no one I can turn to to say 'remember when?' Even if it's a brother or a sister you hate, you know? It's like my past is only unto me and that which I can remember. And my main worry about Madeline, my little girl, is leaving *her* before she's ready . . . and in my present situation [as a recently bereaved daughter] I think part of me is *real resentful*—not toward my mother, but just toward life in general, that I'm at a time when I need her [my mother], Madeline needs her, and we don't have her. I have Dad but, you know, it takes a while to get used to Dad without Mom. I'm so grateful to *him*—but why settle for one when you could have two? I could have had her ten years longer if . . . "

Another constant concern of many late-born children, many still in their twenties and thirties, is how to cope with the frailty of their parents, either at present or as an approaching reality.

Peter Cochran, newly graduated from college and whose parents had recently separated, worried about his mother. "I'm concerned that she's growing older and is approaching the age when she won't be able to do all the things she's accustomed to doing. It's a real worry, and one that's fairly unique." He paused, and then said sharply, "Especially when your peers are all essentially care *free*." These last words were sounded almost explosively, bitterly, as though the thought had been waiting, unacknowledged, and had just surfaced into his consciousness.

"I don't want to make it sound a very negative thing," he quickly added, eager, as he had been throughout his interview, to present older parenting in the best possible light.

And Frank Martin, at only seventeen, worries about his parents' age and how that might affect his future: "As they get older, they seem to have less energy. They seem to have aged considerably over the past years. I'm afraid they may not live until I have graduated from college. And maybe I would have to support either one of them." His concern was of his being "torn in several directions," wanting to earn his degree while being responsible for an aging parent's well-being. "I'm not sure I'm up to the task."

Even Charles Finch, whose memories of childhood are glowing, as are those of Peter Cochran, worries now, at age thirty-eight, about his aging and ailing parents.

"I noticed them aging only relatively recently," Charles told me, "considering my Dad's eighty-two. But, with him, especially, it's been rather stunning, the past two years. He's getting toward, I would say, maybe a little . . . feeble, would be the word." And although he appeared to play down the extent of their aging, wanting to emphasize the positive aspects of late parenting, it was clear he had given considerable thought to his parents' advancing years, their serious health problems, and the care of whichever parent survives the other.

"Well, a lot depends on which one goes first. Frankly, I think within a matter of months after the first one expires, the other will follow. I don't think they could live without one another . . . . If my mother goes first, I would try to have my Dad here, bring him out here to live with me for as long as possible. I have a hunch he may be getting close to the nursing home type of place, where people could keep an eye on him because, every once in a while, he falls and things like that. The couple in *On Golden Pond* are so much like my parents. They're almost a metaphor, Katharine Hepburn, being the stronger of the two. Fortunately, my Dad's a lot nicer than Henry Fonda was in that movie! But he's getting old and, although he doesn't lose his way, he's getting weaker than my mother is. On the other hand, if something happened to *him*, either my mother would come out here or I'd go back there [to a southern state]. Oh yes, I've considered that because, whatever happens, it's going to fall on me."

I spoke to Charles again, a few weeks after our long interview session. He was about to spend two months of the summer break from his university duties with his parents in their home. His mother was undergoing chemotherapy after a mastectomy. He would do what he could for them while he was there, he said, around the house and the yard. And although he hoped to get some of his own work done (was even shipping his typewriter), his major concern was with his parents' well-being. He feared that the cancer, which had now reached her bone marrow, would cause his mother's bones to break.

"If that happens, I think I'll have to find somewhere for them to be together. I don't want them to be separated, and Dad is not able to take care of himself now." His father, he said, was becoming noticeably "more forgetful." "I think I might bring them out here, near me, so that I can visit them all the time."

Clearly Charles' feelings of love and his sense of responsibility for his parents are substantial, even to the extent of rearranging his own life to accommodate his increasingly ailing parents. And while his descriptions of his childhood seemed almost idyllic, he did cite "lack of grandparents" as perhaps the only real drawback of being a late-born child. "I guess one of the disadvantages of having older parents for many of us is it means growing up without grandparents. My first experience, the only close brush with death touching me personally, was when my grandmother died. That was when I was twelve or thirteen. Everybody loved her. And it hit like a lightning bolt. Then my grandfather died. He lived on for quite a while, about five years, and he stayed with us. Not all the time; my mother and her sister took turns. He had arthritis, but he was a marvelous old man and I would help him change and get ready for bed and sit and talk with him. I never knew my father's parents. They were both dead before I was on the scene. So I think maybe lack of grandparents is a disadvantage. On the other hand," he added, still searching for positive comments, "we inherited quite a lot of money from my grandparents, which made my going to the University of M. much easier!"

The joy, brief though it may have been, of knowing an old person, a grandmother or grandfather, intimately, of sharing stories, secrets, not to be divulged to others, of learning old ways, was also spoken of by Rosemary Cross.

"My grandmother was a super baker. I remember to this day my grandmother teaching me how to make apple-peelings tart. She would do the apple tart, and I would get to do the *peelings* tart, which probably tasted awful ... but it was her way of passing on old skills. My grandmother was very ... she wasn't plump, she was *fat* when she died. I think that was because she went blind and sat in a chair and ate pounds of peppermints. She smelled lovely! It was so nice to be hugged by this ... mountain ... of mint!" She laughed at the sweetness of the memory.

Christine Strongman, too, spoke with joy of a childhood warmed and enriched by grandparents:

"My father's parents lived with us from the time I was about six years old, and my mother's mother lived with us, too. It was just marvelous for a kid! I had all those grandparents as a captive audience, particularly my little grandmother who was crippled and who could never leave her room. She would say I was the only one who fluffed her pillows right. She was a marvelous old lady who told me great stories about growing up in Kentucky. She'd tell all the experiences she had as a child in the Civil War .... It was she who instilled my interest in history very very early."

Cheryl Greenham missed her grandparents. "They lived a little while ... but by the time I was four or five, they were dead. I always had a haunting notion—I'd heard wonderful stories about him—that my mother's father was watching over me. And I'd see this vague figure in the distance! I always had a notion he was kinda there, Grandfather Romano. But no. No grandparents," she concluded, wistfully.

Cheryl's father, she remembered, had seemed more grandfatherly than fatherly. "When I was sixteen, he was in his sixties. And he *looked* like a grandfather." He had died two years before, at seventy-seven years of age, after a long illness through which Cheryl had helped nurse him.

"I had gone back to school. I hadn't finished my degree, so I went back and was living quite a bohemian life. It was great! I had my bike and a pair of jeans and some boots . . . . And I had a little job. It was just a simple life. Then mother said that Daddy was pretty sick and that she needed some surgery and would I come home. So I did come home and it was . . . hard. It was hard coming back."

Because her mother was also ill during her father's illness, most of the responsibility for her father's care fell upon Cheryl.

"Mother had to go to the hospital. She had an emergency colostemy—it was just horrendous. I was going to the hospital every day, as well as trying to maintain a difficult relationship with my boyfriend, who was becoming incredibly possessive, and I was trying to take care of Daddy, who had Parkinson's Disease . . . . I had to get his meals and sometimes help him dress. I mean, no one wants to see their father naked. It was hard because he was this little old man who needed nursing and I had to do it. And I resented it. But I did it. Then mother left hospital . . . but had to be taken back . . . . And I got home to find Daddy had fallen out of a chair and broken his hip, so the whole thing began again . . . "

Cheryl felt she was quite young, at twenty-eight years of age, to have to learn the lessons that come with caring for a dying parent.

"I wish I could have . . . well . . . dealt with it better. I really found out a lot about grief. Grief and death is not romantic or pretty. It's ugly, and you get angry and jealous and mad and resentful . . . . You have feelings of love but . . . you know . . . a lot of other emotions come into play. And you're a fool if you think anything else. I didn't know that before."

One way to see one's grandchildren to adulthood, even though one is an older parent, is to choose one's genes carefully and come from exceptionally long-lived stock! Alice Marshall, who contacted me after reading my story in the *Los Angeles Times*, eager to speak positively of being a late-born child, has a mother who, at ninety-one, is still active, alert, busy, and full of life. An aunt, her mother's older sister, died recently at ninety-three and Alice's grandmother, her mother's mother, lived until only three months before her one hundredth birthday. Alice was born when her mother was forty-four. Married young and then divorced, she has two relatively late-born children of her own, born when she was thirty-four and thirty-six years of age. Her husband is six years older than herself.

Alice's father died of a heart attack when he was fifty-nine and Alice was fifteen, but her mother, she feels, provides reassurance to Alice's children, now twelve and fourteen years old, that their mother, too, will be long-lived, just as Alice's own grandmother, in Alice's words, "provided a barrier for me having to deal with my mother's mortality."

At forty-seven, Alice has recently "gone back to school" to train as a psychological counselor. "My mother has been a real inspiration to me. She's made me feel that age is no barrier, that there's plenty of time left for me to do whatever I want to do, to become whatever I can become." Her mother first entered the world of work at sixty-four, lying about her age to get the job she wanted. "She told them she was fifty! She worked for the same company for fifteen years, and then they told her she must retire because she was now sixty-five. Actually, she was seventy-nine! And she still gets a pension for her fifteen years of work!"

Alice realizes that her mother—"traveling in Europe last summer at age ninety" and, at ninety-one, "still going to school, still taking classes"—is exceptional. "When we meet an older person, we have a hard time recognizing that this is how my mother could have been! She's just amazing! She's a wonderful model for me, and for my children."

But, after much admiring talk about her mother, Alice admitted to a lasting resentment over her father's death. She had no opportunity to know him. "He worked so hard and he was gone so often." Now she feels cheated, she says. "If I'd been the first (instead of the last-born child?) I'd have known him longer."

The old Jewish blessing quoted by Ted Martelli at the beginning of this chapter can be bestowed upon very few parents who have their children late, even given the extended life expectancies of modern men and women. Few will live to see their grandchildren married. And the children of older parents are more likely to know their grandparents only fleetingly than are children of younger parents. These are facts of life.

Further, the double generation gap between parents and their late-born children, the gap that puts parents chronologically in the grandparent generation, may have costs for the children that those born to younger parents do not have to meet. Men, whose life expectancy is less than women's, may die before their children reach adulthood. In her book *Father Loss: Women Discuss the Man That Got Away,* Elyce Wakerman has described the painful and long-term effects of father loss on the lives of hundreds of girls. Women consistently spoke of the loss of their fathers as the most signficant event of their lives. Or, if older fathers live, they may have less energy to spare for their children, be less athletic, less boisterous than men twenty years their junior. They may be more like grandfathers than fathers.

Late-born children may find they have ailing parents to care for while they are still in their twenties and thirties, parents as old as their friends' grandparents. The difference is in the "generation between" who will care for their contemporaries' grandparents, should that be necessary.

How important *are* grandparents in children's lives? Studies from the child's viewpoint of this special relationship are relatively few, but the feelings voiced by late-born children interviewed for this book seem to confirm the findings of other researchers that it is richly rewarding. J.F. Robertson, for instance, found that teenagers and young adults who grew up with grandparents relished the relationships and said they would have missed a great deal had they been deprived of them. A. Kornhaber and K.L. Woodward added that when children see and interact with their grandparents, they gain not only a sense of security in the love and understanding their grandparents extend to them but also a sense of family history. To those who have no memories of grandparents, or whose memories of them are dim, the loss seems significant. Contrary to the old saying, "You don't miss what you've never had," people do feel deprived when they have been denied grandparents. Some of those interviewed created their own—the old lady next door, an elderly couple along the street, called upon to serve as surrogates.

Those who knew their grandparents well remember them as providing many kinds of comforts. Christine Strongman, for instance, spoke longer, and more lovingly, about her grandparents than she did about her parents.

"I slept in my grandmother's room. She was the one who really was my champion. Whenever I did anything bad, or that people didn't like, I always ran to my grandmother. She would protect me . . . I was crazy about her. She was the one I wanted to be like."

"Your grandparents, then, seemed very important in your life," I said.

"Well," she answered, "My mother was so tired. And she had lots of things to do."

Charles Finch and Rosemary Cross also relished the time they spent with their grandparents: the companionship, the shared confidences and shared tasks. The love with no strings attached.

Grandparents, for a fortunate few, seem to have served as friends, confidantes, and champions, as well as representing the Omega generation and providing, as Alice Marshall indicated, a barrier against parents' mortality.

5

The Follow-On Late-Born Child

"Little red caboose
Little red caboose
Little red caboose
    Behind the train..."

Some children come into the family after a break, sometimes a long break, between themselves and the next most recently born child and often represent another chance, probably a last-chance, for their parents to hold and enjoy a baby of their own.

The caboose phenomenon is not new. Women sometimes had an unexpected (and not always welcome) addition to their families when they thought it was no longer possible or likely for them to conceive. The "menopause baby" came when its parents prematurely relaxed the use of birth control.

But the caboose phenomenon is also a new trend; as people divorce, change partners, and remarry, so there is a tendency for couples to create "our" child, sometimes in addition to "your" child(ren) or "my" child(ren).

Of the four children of older parents interviewed who were born to fathers or mothers who had been married before, three were only children; only one, David Crenshaw, had older siblings from his then forty-year-old mother's previous marriage. None of the caboose babies in the study perceived himself or herself as an "accident." All eleven felt themselves wanted by their parents and, as such, their feelings about being late-born children are of interest to older couples considering new babies after their earlier children are ten or more years old, whether because of remarriage, or for some other reason.

Margaret Pearce, a petite, youthful woman of forty with boyish cropped hair, met me at the door of her pleasant suburban house dressed in the kind of casual, sporty clothing her young sons might have worn; jeans and a white, sleeveless, V-necked sweater over a brightly checked shirt. She smiled in greeting, but she soon became serious, then sad, as we talked.

She had written an impassioned letter to me after my article on older parents appeared in the *Los Angeles Times*. Among many such statements she wrote, "being the child of older parents was so painful to me that I will *never* parent a child at my age. I could not do that to a child."

Her parents were both close to forty-two years old when Margaret was born; her sister was eleven and her brother was seventeen years of age. She had been a much-wanted child, according to "an elaborate story" her parents told her, one that had been confirmed, she said, by other people who knew her parents at the time.

In 1943, during World War II, her mother went out of state to take care of her niece and her niece's new baby. The young mother's parents had died some time before, and the baby's father was away, serving in the army, so there was no one but Margaret's mother to help the new mother and her infant.

"When my mother came back to my father, she told him, 'It's very nice, holding a baby again and, really, this is our last chance.' So they had me! They worked out an arrangement— interesting, because my father, who had never done any housework, anything that smacked of 'women's work,' agreed to take care of the laundry for the baby and he used to wash my diapers by hand in the basement. My sister tells stories that she would sell tickets to the neighborhood kids to watch through the window!"

"That was really rather advanced for the time," I commented.

"Well, I wonder now if *he* was the one who really wanted the baby and if this was some kind of deal they made with one another. My parents were extremely old-fashioned in their childrearing practices, but my mother was also quite advanced for the time. She didn't believe in staying around the house all day long, cooking and cleaning and playing bridge. She went out and worked. She ran my father's office—he was a publisher—and she had worked when her other children were little, too."

"In what ways, then, were your parents old-fashioned?"

"Well their attitudes were totally different from contemporary parents' attitudes, and from those of parents of my friends. Their approach to life was different . . . there was really *no* parenting. It was that children performed, did what their parents wanted them to do, and never caused any trouble. The positive side of that was that I was given quite a lot of freedom. I was expected to make up my own mind and choose the things I wanted to do. If I could convince them that what I wanted to do was valid, they would let me do it, although they rarely, if ever, participated in any of the events I was interested in, any clubs . . . they were not involved."

"Why do you thing that was? Simply because they were older or . . . ?"

"I think it was a combination of the fact that they were so much older, and that they'd already had children. If they had ever had any desires to do things with their children, they'd already done them with their older children."

"They weren't terribly old people, really."

"Oh, but they *seemed* old. They seemed very old. I'm forty now, so I realize that, no, they weren't terribly old and were perfectly capable of copulation and of having sex appeal for each other. That was something I could never understand." She laughed. "How could they have done that when they were so *old*?" she paused, and then continued.

"My sister says my mother didn't spend much time with her, either. It was as if my parents didn't feel they had to do things with their kids."

"Perhaps, then, it was less to do with age," I suggested, "than with view of life."

"Yes, but you see my mother's view of life was triggered by the fact of her age. Perhaps, when my sister was young, and my mother was young, and all of my sister's friends' parents were young, they may have all felt the same way . . . but my mother was, for *me* different from my friends' parents. Even though some of their mothers worked, and some didn't, they all would do . . . the things we do with our kids now and think nothing of it. You know, go off to ball games and whatever. I did go to those things. My friends' parents would take me. It was never my parents . . . . My mother was never a Brownie leader or anything like that, although I belonged to a lot of things."

"Do you really think that was because of their age, or because of the kinds of people they were?" I asked again.

"Well, they were involved in other things by then. They were grandparents by the time I was a Brownie, so that any extra energy they had went toward being grandparents."

It was in talking about her brother and sister that Margaret lost her composure. At first, she battled her tears, sniffing discreetly and patting her eyes with a tissue. Finally, she began sobbing uncontrollably and was unable to continue our discussion for several minutes. At intervals, thereafter, she stopped talking, her throat too constricted to continue.

"My sister's eleven years older than I am and she was, in reality, a surrogate mother and is now a surrogate grandmother to my kids."

"Did you like her?" I asked

"Yes. I loved her."

"And did she tell you what to do? Did she give orders? Or was she simply there for you to turn to?"

"She was just always there. She took care of me. She was the one who told me the facts of life. I mean, my mother didn't... You know... my mother wasn't... able to, I guess." She stopped for a few moments. "I guess I have some real resentments about this." She paused, again.

"My brother," she began again, "was so much older than I was.... It was as though we were a separate family. He and I have no relationship. He was out of the house... went away to college when I was about six months old and he never really came back. He got married soon after college, so he always had his own house. It's not as if I have any memories of him." Her voice was shaking.

"Do you get along with him now?"

"We don't *not* get along. We just don't get along."

"You mean you don't know each other?"

"Yes. We pass polite conversation, just as you would with a stranger."

"One might have thought he'd be enchanted with the new baby in the house...," I began.

"No!" Her tone was sharp. "Perhaps if he'd been a couple of years younger... if he had spent... a bit of time... And then, when I was eight years old, he had his own child, so I was an eight-year-old aunt. And any enchantment he was going to have about children was directed toward his own children."

Again, she stopped talking. Tears formed and ran down her face.

"I'm sorry that I missed..." She was unable to continue.

"Having a brother?" I prompted.

"Well, yes. It's only since I've turned forty... it's as though I've passed a milestone, and I've been thinking about it an awful lot."

"What do you think sparked it off?" I asked.

"I think it's because my parents are doing so poorly." Her voice was thin and tearful.

"They must be quite old, now. In their eighties."

"Yes, they're eighty-two. My mother has been diagnosed as having Alzheimer's disease and my father is taking care of her but not really doing a very good job. He's not doing a good job of taking care of himself . . . so . . . I'm feeling very bad about the whole family situation. It's my brother who lives near them (on the East coast) so he's the one in charge . . . and so . . . my lack of closeness to him has come to the forefront again. Because I would like to be able to talk to him about what's going on with the parents, and I'm not."

"Can't you . . . What happens if you just call him?"

"Oh, he simply doesn't talk about it. He has his own problems with it."

"Well, he's nearby . . . "

"Yep. He's nearby. So he feels it's his responsibility and not anybody else's."

Added to the deep sorrow Margaret feels about the distance between herself and her brother is regret that the same kind of distance exists between her children and her brother's and sister's children.

"My kids, they're so much younger than their cousins, my nephews and nieces, it's as if they don't have any cousins their own age. It's the whole thing repeated all over again!"

Alice Marshall, whose father died when she was fifteen, found, unlike Margaret, some real advantages in being the last in a family of three children:

"When my father died, neither of my brothers was living at home, but the eldest came back. He was working out of state and he moved back home. That was very comforting. Having this older brother, eight and a half years older than me, was a comfort when I was growing up. It wasn't that I had an intimate relationship with either of my brothers—certainly not with my older brother, the one who came home to replace my father's role, so to speak. He was almost a stranger to me. He'd left home to join the navy when I was young and from the navy he went to college, and from college he went to work a thousand miles away. So when he appeared suddenly, it was as though I had discovered this wonderful older brother that I would be able to depend upon. But I didn't have an intimate relationship with him."

The lack of intimacy with the brother nearly nine years older than herself did not seem to cause her the kind of pain that Margaret Pearce felt at a similar lack of closeness. Rather:

"What I mean by 'comfort' was the reality of knowing that I *had* an older brother and knowing that, if anything happened to my parents, the responsibility would not fall on me. I would not be expected to survive on my own."

In fact, Alice's mother, in whom, Alice said, she sensed a great fear for her only daughter—partly because Alice had been a victim of polio as a child and was left with some minor handicaps—had made provision for Alice in the only way she could:

"She sometimes put it to me that my brothers had reassured her that she need not worry. If anything should happen to her and I was not married, if I had any needs, they would be there for me. It was a way of satisfying *herself,* I suppose. But it was very reassuring to me."

Just as Margaret Pearce's sister served as "a surrogate mother," so other caboose babies, like Charles Finch, also felt they had *two* mothers, one young and one much older.

Charles Finch, a university teacher, thirty-eight years old when interviewed, was born when his mother was herself thirty-eight, his father forty-four. His sister had then just celebrated her thirteenth birthday. His mother, Charles told me, had suffered a miscarriage between the two births and both she and his father had been ecstatic when he was born. Speaking at length and only positively about growing up with older parents, Charles felt, he said, "extra lucky" at having a much older sister.

"She adored me! Still does, I assume. In a way, one reason I'm in academe today is that she was in college when I was five or six years old so, while other kids were watching Captain Video, I was drawing maps of the Roman Empire and reading her college text books when she came home. She got a good bit of limelight, but she always made sure I was a part of everything. She refused to go out with people if she felt she'd been out too much and wasn't paying enough attention to me . . . . She functioned almost as a third parent."

Charles Finch's older sister, then, was surrogate mother, role model, and caring friend.

For Ted Martelli, too, born to even older parents than Charles Finch, one sister was particularly important to his young life. Ted's mother and father, Italian immigrants, were forty-two and fifty years old when he was born, forty-two years ago, after three sisters who were ten, fourteen, and fifteen years older than he. There had been another boy, his parents' firstborn, also named Ted, who was killed when eight years old in a car accident.

"My middle sister, Nancy, was very maternal to me and I always felt she was bringing me up. She died this past year at sixty, I think . . . fifty-nine or sixty." He wasn't sure. "When I was five or six, she was around nineteen. So she was a young woman at the time. I just remember her as almost maternal. In addition, my mother was quite ill when I was growing up, so my sister was a kind of surrogate mother to me. She was the only one of my sisters who went to college."

Ted, too, eventually went to college and, in fact, earned a doctorate, to become the first professional in his family but, although his emotionally closest sister may have served as a role model and parent surrogate, Ted did not find much comfort in his family of older sisters.

"I was the only boy in this houseful of young women. In some ways it was *more* isolating rather than less. My sisters were quite a bit older than me and they were growing up and dating at the time I was a baby . . . and one of them went off to college and the others went to work young. As I say, one of them spent a lot of time with me, but the others . . . I didn't really have much contact with them."

The caboose babies in this study often pointed to the lack of contact they had with their older siblings. David Crenshaw hardly knew his older half-brother and sister, fifteen and eleven years his senior. "Well, to be quite honest, it's a relation in name only. There was such an age difference. [My brother] was gone to college three years after I was born. My sister and I were a little closer . . . but, then she moved away. We haven't kept in close touch." For David, this seems not to have been a great deprivation. He spoke of having been a happy child who "always had someone . . . . I always had someone at home. That made the difference."

But Frank Martin, the youngest of the interviewees (seventeen years old), whose sister is nineteen years his senior, regrets the lack of closeness between them. "My relationship with her is about the same as with my parents. We're distant. I love my sister . . . but we have nothing in common." Like several of the less happy late-born children, Frank spoke often of his longing for more closeness within his family.

Jim Compton, twenty, has a sister ten years older, and two brothers sixteen and nineteen years older, than he is.
"Only my sister was at home when I was little. My brothers were both away at college at the time and after that . . . well, I hardly knew them. I never really grew up with them at all."
Asked if he felt close to his brothers now, Jim said, "No. Not very. There's that big age difference. I never really got close to them. They were either at college or in the army. We never really had a brotherly relationship."
Jim did, however, feel close to his sister who, now married and with three children of her own, lives with her family in the same apartment building as Jim and his parents.

"My mother has always gone out to work, but I didn't mind because my sister was at home when I was, and I enjoyed being with my sister. So I didn't think about my mother being out."

And, unlike Margaret Pearce, whose older brother made her an aunt at eight years old, and who felt hurt and resentful at her brother's seeming abandonment or transference of any interest he may had in her to his own child, Jim finds real delight in being uncle to a twelve-year-old. The child was born when Jim was eight, just as Margaret had been when her brother's child was born.

"He's been kinda like a little brother to me." Jim said. "He was always around. So he's been kinda like the little brother I never had. I've got someone I can teach things to, and play with. It's like I wasn't deprived of a younger brother."

Even with sisters twenty and seven years older than herself, and brothers sixteen and twelve years her senior, Barbara Anderson felt herself neglected by her parents and by her siblings—and experienced little pleasure at being an aunt to a niece just one year younger than herself. Between her and her closest-in-age sister "there was some kind of . . . odd rivalry. She and I hated each other for years." She laughed. "I think it may have been that she was the baby for so long and then I came along and kind of distorted everything. She was the one who always told on me. She always sided with my parents against me." As a child, she says, she felt lonely and unloved. "By the time I was born, my [older] sister was already out of the house and married. And my brother was in the navy. So we were very scattered. There was not a lot of family cohesiveness at all."

Her parents, Barbara recalls, had little time or energy for her, her mother, who had been forty years old when Barbara was born, constantly foisting her on her older sister and her older sister's child. "But," Barbara insisted, "it wasn't that I felt I had *two* mothers but, rather, as though I didn't *have* a mother, per se. My sister kind of got me by default. Now, she *would* play with us, my niece and me. She made up songs for us and she painted my niece's room with great murals of Winnie the Pooh and ... actually, I was very jealous of her [my niece]. I mean, she seemed to have more of a child's life than I did. I was forced to behave like a grown up more often and I felt very alienated, especially from my niece, because she was a child. Even though the age difference between us is very small, we had entirely different personalities and development. I knew that, even then. She could do different things. She could listen to Little Toot [?] and Tubby the Tuba, and she had a room with a great picture of Winnie the Pooh, and she had games around and dolls, and did things with her Mom ... went to the beach ... and they made rock people together. And I remember, when I was at their house, I would do that as well. I liked it much more than I did at my house because we did things with my sister—we went to the beach, we went for drives."

"Was that a comfort, in some ways?" I asked.

"Yes. But it was also uncomfortable. It was 'well, why isn't *my* life like this?' It seemed ideal; it was something I desired ... and I feel now that my parents didn't pursue a relationship with me ... and that may have been because I spent so much time with my sister and her family, now that I think about it."

Now, at twenty-three, Barbara feels closer to her brothers and sisters than she did as a child. "All my siblings have expressed compassion for my being in the position I was because my parents were so advanced in age, compared to theirs, and they were kind of tired of raising kids by the time they got to me." She has finally developed a good relationship, she says, with the younger of her two sisters; her dealings with her parents remain strained and antagonistic, although she says she is trying to resolve some of her resentments toward them.

Christine Strongman, at fifty-four years old the oldest person in the study, was the last of four children. Her brother was ten years older and her sisters eight and five years older than she. Her older sister served as surrogate mother.

"By that time," she said, "my mother was so tired, she just turned me over to my sister."

She and her older sister had a somewhat turbulent relationship when Christine was young: "We would get into fights . . . constantly arguing. I'd always say, 'you're not my mother! You can't tell me what to do!' "

But, in spite of the fights and arguments, Christine was close to both her sisters and has remained close to them, emotionally and geographically, all her life. It was her sisters who helped launch all three girls into a singing career, taking Christine, then still a schoolgirl, touring on the road, caring for her, and assuming full adult responsibility for her.

Between Christine and her much older brother, again, the distance of years could not be easily spanned. Her conversation bubbled when she spoke of her sisters, but her brother was hardly mentioned.

One child of older parents in this study feels she had more than one surrogate parent! Sylvia Shaw was the last child in a family of four girls. Her sisters were thirteen, ten, and two-and-a-half years old when she was born, so the family comprised two sets of girls, Sylvia and the sister closest to her age forming a double caboose. These two late babies were born in 1945 and 1948, after their father returned from years away from home, serving with the military.

"There seemed to be older sisters always at home," she said. "One would go to college, leaving the other at home. When the other went to college, the first one returned home . . . *All* my sisters treated me like their daughter! And who wants four mothers in one home!" She laughed as she spoke, seeming to bear no animosity toward her bossy sisters.

Her sisters lived at home after finishing college: "The house was filled with mother substitutes," Sylvia continued. "It didn't escape me that my older sisters in their twenties looked like some of my friends' mothers! I was awful to them" she confessed, again laughing, "and called them 'old maids' and other disparaging terms. I was a horrid little kid!"

Most people are familiar with the term "sibling rivalry" and researchers may have tended to emphasize the negative aspects of the relationship. While it is true that brothers and sisters are in competition with each other for attention from their parents, particularly their mother, substantial child development literature does focus on the positive aspects as well. The evidence is that, although they may be rivals, children generally enjoy being with their brothers and sisters. Through their interactions, they learn from each other, they influence each other's interests. An early study by Rudolph Schaffer and Peggy Emerson suggests that many babies grow attached to older siblings, miss them when they are gone, are happy to see them, and prefer them to other children as playmates. And older siblings, according to Debra Pepler, often teach younger children many kinds of skills, including the use of words and numbers and how to play with toys and games and so on. Urie Bronfenbrenner, too, agrees that interactions with older children are a major way children develop social traits and learn mutual cooperation.

For caboose babies Alice Marshall, Charles Finch, Jim Compton, and Christine Strongman, having a substantially older sibling, a sister, was comforting. Margaret Pearce, though, feels hurt and resentment over the large age differences between herself and her siblings, even though her older sister, whom she loved, and still loves dearly, played a maternal role toward her. Ted Martelli, appreciative of his middle sister's part in his upbringing, nevertheless found a houseful of older sisters "isolating." Barbara Anderson, who spent a great deal of time with her married sister and her sister's child, was anguished by the contrast between her sister's parenting style and that of her mother. This, at the same time as she liked being at her sister's house much more than being at her own house. Most of the caboose babies experience, and regret, some emotional distance between themselves and some of their older siblings.

As was seen earlier, Margaret Pearce, Ted Martelli, Barbara Anderson, and Frank Martin, all perceive their childhood years as less happy, less satisfying, than do the other caboose babies. Many elements, of course, enter into a child's sense of his or her happiness, but the nature of the relationships with older siblings does appear to carry some weight. Perhaps parents can help make these relationships closer, more comforting.

Alice Marshall's mother surprised Alice when she indicated her feeling of not having much to give to her daughter:

"When I told my mother you were coming to interview me about what it's like to be the child of an older mother, she thought for a little while, and then she said, 'I guess you'll have to tell her you learned everything on your own.' Can you believe that? She, who's taught me so much!"

Her mother, foreign born and without much formal education, appears to have shown unusual wisdom and perception in some aspects of her childrearing. Perhaps she was, as Alice suggested, merely trying to ease her own concerns about her daughter's well-being, but her gentle reminders to Alice that her brothers, though far away, cared about her, and would take care *of* her, should Alice be in need, provided a sense of security for the girl, provided one more support in the structure of supports making for emotional good health. Alice feels that, ideally, children should be born close together, to share each other— her own children were born only two years apart. She did not know a real intimacy with her brothers but neither did she resent them. Rather, she was grateful they were there, assured that, somewhere in the world, they were ready to protect her if needed.

How much of the lifelong closeness between Charles Finch and his older sister was influenced or encouraged by their parents, Charles did not say but his memories of his early years indicate an unusually close, loving, and giving family, each member of which was proud of each of the others and who treated each other gently and with courtesy. Even when she became a college student, his sister continued to devote time to the little boy, careful not to neglect him. One could assume that the parents' behavior toward the children provided a model of behavior for the daughter to emulate.

Barbara Anderson, on the other hand, feels her parents abandoned her to her older sister, and Margaret Pearce also feels that her parents did *no* parenting. With their older children grown up, they devoted themselves more fully than ever to their work, leaving Margaret to make her own decisions, participating little in her childhood activities, and abrogating most of their responsibility for childrearing to their older daughter. Then, heaping what Margaret perceived as neglect upon neglect, they lavished such interest as they had in young children on their grandchild, the child of their firstborn, unwittingly hammering in even further the wedge dividing Margaret from her brother. Margaret, though, has remained close to her sister who was "just always there," just as Ted Martelli remained close to his middle sister until she died.

Sylvia Shaw and Christine Strongman both fought and argued with their older sisters in what might be seen as normal family give-and-take, as one member sought to exert what she felt to be her proper authority and the other struggled for independence. This was so for Celia Abbott, another caboose baby whose comments are not cited here because they so often duplicated those cited by other such children. Sylvia Shaw, Christine Strongman, and Celia Abbott express no "regret" or "sorrow" about their childhood relationships with their older siblings and all say they have fond and caring relationships with them now.

As will be seen in other places in this book, children appear to need a sense of security, a sense that significant people in their lives care about them, if they are to be happy. They need others to speak to, to confide in. They need caring others to guide them, not oppressively but with affectionate firmness. They need to feel they are not alone.

The caboose baby has others, usually caring others, to meet these needs. The majority of the now adult caboose babies who tell their stories here, perceive their childhood years as normally happy, their needs having been met by older siblings, among other people. When a child discerns, though, that its parents abandon their responsibilities to others, even if it be to other children, he or she may be left with lifelong feelings of anger and resentment.

6

Attitudes Toward Late-Parenting

The proof of the pudding is in the eating.—Cervantes

One way, perhaps the surest way, to assess the satisfaction of children of older parents is to ask them: Would you choose late-parenting for yourself, or recommend it to others?

Only five of the twenty-two late-born children interviewed for this book had chosen, or said they would choose, to have their children "late," and only two of those expressed unqualified enthusiasm for the choice.

Cheryl Greenham, thirty years old and as yet unmarried, has many reservations about late parenting. Her mother was forty-three when Cheryl was born and her father, who was forty-eight, had found it difficult to talk to his child across that wide age gap.

"I think if people consider having children at an older age—and it looks like the sins of the fathers revisited; it looks like I'm going to have children at a late age—I think they should learn to play with their children, and include them . . . and *do* things with them. Become children themselves again. It won't hurt.

"I also think it would be beneficial to communicate with

those kids and tell them what's going on. I mean 'You *are* different. You do have parents that are older, and if you talk to me about it, come to me about . . . let's be friends. Let's communicate!' I know, myself, as a teacher, I find it's easier when I stop treating kids like kids and just communicate with them. Children today are very sophisticated, so they can handle it. But they can't handle you not being straight with them. It means working extra hard to develop that extra rapport with the children when there's a substantial age gap."

If Cheryl doesn't see any real advantage for the children of older parents, she does think there are advantages for the parents.

"After living together the last couple of years, since Daddy died, mother and I have really quite open, friendly communication. I think, living round me, she's just got groovier. I mean, she's had to step it up. And she's really aware . . . she's made lots of younger friends of her own."

If she has children in her late thirties, as her mother was when Cheryl was born, she will behave differently from the way her parents behaved. "I think I would want it to be more *fun!*" she said, laughing. "And with children in their teens when you're getting into your fifties . . . well, I guess that's cause to try and stay as fit and healthy as you can."

Cheryl, like many young women today, entering her thirties, unmarried and not sure she will find a suitable husband, has thought about "just having a baby, someday . . . but," she added, "I know what it was like to go through . . . without much from Daddy. And I don't know if I'd wish that on a child . . . . But, at the same time, I'd sure hate to be denied that experience. Still, I've had kids in my classes who have only their mothers . . . and I know how tough it is for them . . . . They do all kinds of weird things, attention-getting things . . . they so much want attention."

Charles Finch, unmarried at thirty-eight, was one of only two of those interviewed to recommend late parenting without any reservations. But he will probably not have children himself, he says, even if he does marry. He professes not to care for children at all.

Because he feels his was a privileged childhood, he believes that older, established couples make better parents than young couples just starting their lives together, for whom he sees children as an "enormous burden." His middle-class values lead him to see having children before being able to afford a house, cars, and other possessions considered necessary to the "good life" as foolish, even irresponsible.

"I'm all for people in their late thirties, even their forties, having children if they want to, if they've got the means to have them and raise them. I think you go through a number of changes as you go through your twenties, particularly now-adays, with the job market being what it is, you're in for a rocky time during your twenties. During their thirties, I think, a lot of people mellow out. So many times my parents said, when talking to other people, 'We really enjoyed having him!' They were able to relax a little bit and just sit back . . . I mean, they were involved with me a lot of the time, but they were really able to enjoy me.

"And, again, as I've said before, the chances are that somewhat older parents will have bigger economic resources and what with it costing, I think, at least $100,000 . . . I think the last I saw was $130,000 to raise a child in a minimal middle-class way these days, I think that has to be taken into account. I get very angry when I see people who have no economic means having child after child after child . . . I think a lot of us want to be able to give our kids at least what we had . . . and that means money. I think we have a lot of evidence that kids are very aware of the social standing of their parents at a very early age. And are very aware when they can't have things.

"My own nephews and nieces have been raised on a very, very limited budget and they couldn't do an awful lot of things. And I can see that has scarred them for life. I do think money and stuff like that does make a difference. And all things being equal, when parents are a little bit older, they're going to have a little bit more and they'll be able to provide those kinds of things. Of course, today, to give your kids things of comparable middle- or upper middle-class upbringing [to what we had], you've got to sit back and think the moment you're conceiving your child, 'What about college?' Middle-class people tend to be future-oriented... I guess that's why so many people I know are either having zero kids, or one child, and I think it's a shame. I hope some of them will reconsider and have late children. It's going to be a terrible waste if they don't. They would make good parents; they're stable people. I don't think I ever will have children, but I would make a much better parent starting in my mid-thirties than I would have in my twenties.

"Again, I think, to some extent, when you're older, you're wiser. I've noticed, reading studies about child abuse and corporal punishment, that older people get less abusive toward kids. One of the major findings in one of the biggest studies of family violence is that older people seem to be less of the opinion that physical punishment is necessary. Maybe it's because it just doesn't work very well... and that the parents are a little older and mellower. I think, again, social class [is important]. In a way, age can be a very positive thing."

Jean Smythe, an only and lonely child of a single mother forty-three years older than herself, was strong in her disapproval of women having babies late in their childbearing years. She was sixteen years old when she married and nineteen when her first child was born, her second child following within a few years.

"Do you have any regrets," I asked her, "about having had your children so early?"

"Oh, *no!*" she answered without hesitation.

"Do you think you were ready for motherhood?"

"Certainly, I was ready for biological motherhood. I wanted my children and I wanted to be young with them. I wanted to do all the things I did with them. I wanted to be energetic, and

I *was*. I was strongly motivated to make my own family and I'm glad that I did and I would do it again. I wish I could have afforded to have more."

"One of the things that leads women to delay childbearing these days is that having a child early interferes with their making gains in their careers," I said.

"So I've heard." Her tone was frosty. Although a career scientist, herself, she has little sympathy with the notion of "careers." "I feel life is more than a career," she said." "A career is only part of life. Ultimately, we are all living lives, not having careers. I'm really surprised," she went on, "that these supposedly bright people don't think ahead. Having a baby is like having another Mercedes to them. Now-or-never Mommies are a new breed. They have a cold view of raising children." She shuddered, to emphasise the coldness. "It's so calculating . . . all that cultural ideology about what parents should be able to provide . . . socioeconomic status! Kids don't give a damn about that! These women, who are supposedly middle-class professional women, women who think, who read, who have abstract minds . . . I would *never* . . . . Or I would adopt."

"Why do you feel that way?" I asked. "If now, at thirty-seven, as you are, you just wouldn't contemplate being a first-time mother? How much of that is to do with being the child of such a mother yourself, and how much has to do with something else?"

"It has a lot to do with that fact. It may be the most significant fact of my early life."

Jean did know someone who had a child in her forties, "Before it was fashionable," whose son, now in his late teens, appears well-balanced and happy. "I shouldn't speak so strongly, perhaps," she concluded, perhaps regretting her earlier, stronger statements. "I suppose it depends on the circumstances."

Marilyn Henry, whose mother was thirty-eight when Marilyn was born, and who is now herself thirty-eight years old, waited ten years after her marriage, until she was thirty-two, to have her own child.

She had not consciously wanted to repeat her mother's choice, she said, and has some regrets, now, that she waited so long. She wanted to become established in her career before making a commitment to a child.

"I worried about it too much .... I know now that it didn't need to be a worry. What worried me, I think, was the whole idea that you have babies *or* you work, but you can't do both and, if you have a baby, you have to be prepared to give up the work. I feel so sad for people who've decided *not* to do it. I shouldn't have hesitated. My daughter is my greatest achievement and my greatest joy."

Marilyn and her husband have decided, though, that they will have no more children.

"I don't know how I would manage with two. Just the doctor's appointments and being Brownie mother of the month . . . I couldn't do it for two."

Marilyn has, for some years, held down a responsible administrative job. She stayed at home with her new baby for a few months and then found a full-time child-minder to care for the child in her own home so that she could go back to work. The same woman has been serving the family for over six years. Even though Marilyn's daughter is now nearly seven years old and in school, the babysitter-cum-housekeeper still arrives at seven in the morning and does not leave until six in the evening, when Marilyn arrives home from work.

"There's not a whole lot of money left out of my check after the babysitter is paid!"

Marilyn feels considerable empathy for her child, having been born to an older mother herself.

"The other evening, in the bath, my daughter asked, 'Mommy, when are you going to die?' and I knew it was her grandma's death a few months ago that prompted the question. A moment or two later she looked at my hair and asked, 'Did *grandma* have gray hair when you were *my* age?' She was trying to benchmark it, I think. Trying to assess how long she'd have me. I know how that feels. I can remember worrying in the same way."

One of the positive aspects of late parenting, Marilyn feels, is that "there's that many more years of wisdom to offer that new young mind." Another is that, with both parents established in careers, "You don't hesitate to buy something . . . for the child."

Peter Cochran, now twenty-two, like his parents, will wait to have children of his own. He sees his own older parents as having provided him with both material things and with intellectual stimulation, and he considers that directly due to their maturity. His reasons for considering late-parenting for himself, however, are largely because of his strong need to establish himself in his career. He perceives the early years in an academic setting as so demanding and so time-consuming as to preclude the possibility of giving children the attention they need.

"At our school," he began, speaking of the small, private college from which he was about to graduate, "there's a woman, a talented molecular biologist who, at forty, just had her second child. This is a woman who has competed for National Institute of Health grants and won them. Not an easy task. She's gotten funds from the National Science Foundation, published in scholarly journals, published text books . . . . And, at forty, she and her husband decided that having another child was what they wanted to do.

"But there are other women on the faculty who at . . . God! Dr. Riverton must be thirty-three or thirty-four, and she's fighting for a tenured spot and knows there is no way she can have a child right now. And I feel for her position. And I also know male professors who, in their mid-thirties, have to make a decision with their wives whether or not they are going to have children because their career is very time consuming . . . . And I realize it's a very difficult decision to make. I won't set myself on a timetable, but I certainly wouldn't start having children until *well* after thirty. I would want to devote time to my children, the way my parents did .... To have a child in my twenties ... it would mean a lot of sacrifice for me. In my thirties, there would be sacrifices, but not in terms of some of the activities I would be pursuing. Then, I think having a child would come more easily."

Young Frank Martin, at seventeen, although expressing strong reservations about having older parents, feeling the substantial age difference acts as a barrier to understanding between them, will, he feels, wait to be a parent until his middle thirties. Like Peter Cochran, he has ambitions that he believes will require his full attention. "I want to establish myself in a career first." He is sure he will be able to build bridges rather than barriers between himself and his children. "I would talk to them more. I would open up. I would praise them, provide a good life for them. School would be my prime concern."

Meg Perkins, twenty-five, an only child, feels that her parents' age was not especially important to her childhood years and has some recommendations for people contemplating having children relatively late in their lives.

"It's really the same advice I would give anybody, whatever their age. I think the difference between a kid being happy or not has to do with being able to spend a lot of good, quality time with the kid and having other kids around. Really, the main thing I missed was having either a brother or a sister ... and more kids around the neighborhood that I could go play with. Kids need other people of *all* ages."

"For yourself," I asked her, "do you think it would be a good time to have a child as late as at thirty-six years of age?"

She laughed. "That's probably when I'll end up having a child—if I do at all. I can't see it for another ten years."

"Why is that?" I probed.

"Because there are other things I want to do first ... and I'm moving into a new job now, in a new industry, so I just don't see it. At *least*, I'll be over thirty."

"So you'll definitely be following the trend?"

"Right! If I'm going to have a child, if anybody's going to have a child, that child should be the *main thing*, I think. I don't know that I could be one of those superwomen who could juggle with a career and a baby."

Jim Compton feel his was a happy, privileged childhood, with caring parents who spent time with him, an older sister who was, and still is, his friend and mentor, and many aunts and uncles for whom he felt considerable affection. But although he was eager to express all the positive aspects of growing up with older parents, when I asked him if *he* would wait until his middle or late thirties to have a family, or if he would recommend others to have babies later in life, he promptly answered, "No! I don't think I would."

"Why wouldn't you," I asked.

"Because, for as long as I can remember, I've always wanted to have a family when I was young, so I could enjoy my kids when I was still active. I always wanted to get married at twenty-one . . . " he laughed, " . . . but as I am getting closer to twenty-one, I guess I'm not going to be married so young. But I *would* like to be married by the time I'm twenty-six or so, and start a family."

"Is that because of what you experienced as a child?"

"Yes"

"So, in some ways, you regret having older parents?"

"Right! That's the only regret I have, that my parents couldn't be as active as I would have liked. They *were* active," he insisted, "but for the most part they weren't, you know, getting out or wrestling with me . . . "

"You mean, you missed the physical horseplay that younger parents have with their children? Rolling around on the floor with their kids?"

"That's exactly what I mean," he agreed. "And I want that for myself and my kids . . . . My sister, she married *very* young, still in her teens, and had her children very young . . . I like that better." This was a similar answer to that of David Crenshaw who, like Jim Compton, perceives himself to have been a happy child with devoted parents. "Having a choice, I would have children younger. I would have all the children that I cared to have by the age of thirty-five. I would still want to be young enough and strong enough to be out, to do things outside, especially if I had boys, just to be active. That was something I missed. There's no dodging that, and it's important. When I have children, I want to be able to keep up." He added another reason for choosing younger parenting. "This is thinking way ahead—but when they would become the age of having children, I would still be around to be a grandparent. I missed that and I want to break the trend."

Ted Martelli, now forty-six, has two sons, aged seventeen and sixteen. Ted has thought many times about having more children late in life.

"I haven't really thought about acting on it, though, because I think it gives one the tendency to rely on one's children for one's future. I think that people [men] who have children in their fifties are people who are trying to find a new lease on life, sort of re-energize their lives. Because there are very fond memories of having earlier children. I think there's nothing in life that gives one a stronger sense of drive and purpose than when you first have children. A tremendous sort of euphoria comes over one's life . . . suddenly you have a point and a mission and a purpose and, in the early years of raising children, I think that's very keen. As your children get older and as they move away from you, there's a sense that something is lost in life and it doesn't seem as urgent as it seemed when you were first having children. So, I sometimes think, well, gee, wouldn't it be nice to have another little baby around the house and how exciting that would be! *But*, I always think of that with the

realization that that's not such a necessarily *healthy* way to energize one's later life ... because it's sort of reliving the past
that one cherishes, instead of moving into another phase of life
and finding value in that particular age."

"Do you think you might feel differently if you hadn't
already had children," I asked.

"Well, that would be altogether different ... I'm a very
child-oriented person and I do see children as absolutely essential in one's life. I would have had a hard time had I not had
children until this time. I certainly would have wanted to have
them sometime."

"Given your experiences as the child of older parents, what
might you say to those who are waiting to start a family until
their late thirties and forties?"

Ted pondered for a few moments before answering.

"Well, the reality is, if you're not having your children until
your forties, and even later, that you are probably going to
share much less of your children's lives. You are probably going
to die while your children are still young people. You are probably going to have less chance of seeing your grandchildren. I
don't think that people who put off having children really acknowledge those facts much. The feeling is, well, I'm in my career; I want to do this first; I'll have children after I'm established or after I've done what I want to do. And I don't think
there is a realization that that means your whole relationship
with your children will be quite different from the way it would
be if you'd had children in your twenties and that your children
were twenty years old when you're forty, when you have a kind
of adult relationship with them ... and you're not likely to
know their children." He paused to consider, and then continued.

"If I were advising older, would-be parents about how to in-
sure their child, or children, would have as few problems as
possible, one of the things, I guess, would be to be sure they
continue to take an active role in their child's life as the child is
growing up ... to not ... sort of retire away from it. I dun-

no ... at that point, it seems almost too late to give advice. I think the advice. ... People should think about this earlier in their lives, in the sense of deciding whether, indeed, they really do want to have children late in life, understanding what the consequences are." His words trailed away and he considered the question again.

"It seems to me," he began once more, "that people put off having children because they want to establish careers or do some other thing first. But the problem is, I think, that if you are at all successful in your career, the ages between forty and fifty-five, or thirty-five and fifty-five, are the peak years of involvement ... and that you are going to be very busy in those years with your work and will probably have less time, then, to devote to a child than you would have had in your twenties."

"And you are saying," I suggested, "that children really need time, that you need to spend time with the children?"

"Yes, I think it's essential that you spend time with your children. I have ... certain regrets that my father didn't spend more time with me, although he had a lot of time on his hands. ... Yes. children need and want parents' time ... "

Margaret Pearce was not happy as a child and can still be moved to tears by her unresolved resentment and ambivalence toward her parents and her much older brother. She has powerful reservations about late parenting.

"I'm forty, and I have no intention of having [any more] children because I don't have the energy level that I had when I was twenty-five, and I don't think. ... It may be that I would be a *better* mother, but I don't think I would be the same *kind* of mother. I couldn't spend any time, you know, taking little kids for walks and going to the park and things like that, that I was able to do and wanted to do when my children were little. I had my son in a cooperative nursery, partly because it was cheaper, and also because I wanted to have a very firm grip on what he was doing all the time."

Margaret was twenty-seven years old when her first son was born.

"I was not *that* young, but certainly much younger . . . and I noticed that I did less for my next child—I was thirty-two when he was born—because I was just . . . tired. And wanting to go on to other things. And I think that's part of it . . . both the fact that older parents are tireder—my parents were always tired when I was young—and that they are at a different stage in their lives and want to do other things . . . and the other things may not include dealing with young children."

"Still," I put it to her, "if you'd had no children, as is the case with many career women, if you'd done the whole career bit and were now in your late thirties, say, might you not feel differently?"

"I don't think so. I think what would happen, and what *has* happened to a lot of my friends who have had first children when they were in their late thirties or early forties, is that, yes, they had their career, but they missed their career too much. So they had the child, but then the child got shipped off to daycare as soon as possible and the mother went back to work. That was what they wanted to do at that stage. You know, motherhood is not the be-all and end-all. It's not *all* we can do. It may have been, years ago, all that was expected of us, but that's not the case any longer. And I really feel that, to have a child and not give it the nurturing, not be around for the first tooth and the first step, you're cheating the child; you're cheating yourself."

"Would you have anything to say to would-be older parents?" I asked her. "Given what you know, what would you say . . . 'Great! Have a baby, If that's what you want, have a baby. But let me tell you, from my own experience, what I think you might do to help that child have a happier childhood?' Tell me what you'd say."

"Basically, I would probably say, 'Don't have the baby!' "

"Well, you might think that, but we can't really tell people not to have babies," I suggested, gently.

"I just think that if you cannot be involved with that child's life, if you depend on caretakers.... There's a great deal of pleasure in parenting, in getting involved with the child's activities. It doesn't have to be the only thing in life. I can't imagine anything more boring than your whole life revolving around your children ... but if you're not willing to give your time and energy to your children, then you're not giving either yourself or your child a fair chance, because, in comparison with other children born around the same time, of younger parents, parents who are willing to give of their time, the comparisons will be very bad. Now, that's based on my experience only, and I'm sure you could find other people who have had similar experiences who will say 'I'd rather have been born than not.' "

"I don't think that's the choice," I answered. "The choice is, 'As I've decided to have a baby late in my life, how can I do the right thing, the best thing, by this child?' "

"Yes, but it's difficult to know what the best thing is. A mother who has been a career woman and gives up her career to stay home and take care of the baby may have some resentments, such incredible resentments that she's not doing the baby or herself any favors at all."

When her children were smaller, Margaret did continue to work, but only part time. She returned to full-time work only recently, feeling that it was the right time to do so, now that both her children were older and that safe, city-operated, after-school activities were available for her younger son, now seven years old. She soon returned to part-time work, however, because she felt her full-time employment was having a deleterious effect on the younger boy.

"It got to the point where he was going to school and then going to after-school activities, so he'd be out of the house from eight in the morning until five-thirty in the afternoon, and he didn't like that ... so I started working part time again. He's much happier now ... and I have more energy for the children. I spend a lot of time with them, taking them to soccer practice and being soccer mother, and participating in their clubs and helping them with their school work . . . . You know, there are just so many hours in the day. If you get yourself too fragmented, nobody is helped. And I really feel for those women who feel they *have* to have a child when they're this age. I feel for the kids . . . "

Rebecca Johnson's mother was only thirty-two years old when Rebecca was born, but, as a child, Rebecca perceived her mother as old—older than the mothers of her schoolmates. Her friends' mothers were companions to their daughters, she thought, like older sisters. "And my parents never played with me much. I think they were, maybe, more mature." Her mother, divorced when Rebecca was seven years old, was left in sole care of two children, Rebecca and a brother nineteen months younger than she. She worked outside the home and was left with little time or energy for play with the children, nor did she ever have time to talk with Rebecca. "We never had those kinds of intimate . . . conversations, when we really spoke of emotions . . . and I do feel that had to do with the age difference," Rebecca said. "I hate to say it . . . the lack of intimacy at home . . . seemed to have turned me inwards."

An unhappy little girl, Rebecca never found intimacy with others easy and, at thirty-nine years of age, has never married. She feels that if she did marry, she would not have children.

"I don't know why, but I've never had a desire to have children. It's something I've never really considered."

"Would you recommend late-parenting for others?" I asked her.

"You mean late childbearing? No, I wouldn't. I would recommend against it if I had older friends who were considering it."

"Can you say just why you feel that? Is it based on your own experience? And what do you think is the optimum time to have children?"

"Well, I think the age difference makes it difficult, sometimes, for the parent to relate to the child as well as a younger parent could. Their interests and their interest level maybe so different, so far away, that they aren't able to relate on a childlike level, which I think is important. And I certainly don't mean being childish. I think maybe they can't understand as well where a child is coming from. And it's been too long for them to recall some of the emotions and experiences; they can't understand quite as well as someone who has gone through that not as long ago. My own parents . . . I can't say what their interests were. They didn't seem to have hobbies or those kinds of things. I really can't think of anything that interested them other than their professions and business matters. My Dad . . . frankly, I think he didn't want to have children and take on that responsibility."

"Well, that's certainly different from many couples having late babies now," I suggested. "They are waiting and, when they do have children, they seem to want them very much."

"That's very important, I think" she replied, after considering for a moment. "If I were going to make a recommendation to someone who was older, assuming I had that right and they'd asked my opinion, I think I'd recommend that they make sure they're suited toward having children and that it's something they really want, because they need to make a lifetime commitment . . . certainly until the children are grown up and out on their own. And they need to be sure that there are not other motives for having children that perhaps wouldn't make them good parents. They should really want children, and they should have a good, solid relationship, the potential mother and father. If they don't, they have no business having children."

Rebecca feels keenly the loss of a father's influence in her growing years. She is not in favor of single older women choosing to bear and rear children on their own, a recent trend among career women who have the financial means to support a child on their own.

"Some women I've known have had this tremendous desire

to have a child, as if it's some extention of themselves, some status symbol or something. I think that's terrible . . . . I'd like to see those women, through counseling, be able to deal with that need and resolve it, rather than have a child because of the need. A child is a tremendous responsibility—perhaps it's the greatest responsibility in one's lifetime, to raise a child—and there are so many things that work against doing that successfully. You need to have all your aces lined up, do a lot of homework and a lot of thinking before you do that."

Rebecca does understand the desire of many women to have a profession as well as to rear children. "But," she said, "if they want the two, they are asking for trouble. I'm sure there *are* women who are doing it successfully, but I think they are the lucky ones."

Alice Marshall is, herself, a relatively late-starting parent. She was thirty-four, then thirty-six, when her two children were born, having been previously married and divorced. She is now close to forty-eight and her husband is fifty-three years old. Her children are thirteen and fifteen.

Because her own mother, now ninety-one years old, was, and still is, remarkably active for her age, Alice has never felt that age alone is of great signficance. She recognizes that she is fortunate that her mother has always been healthy and capable, characteristics especially important when her husband died of a heart attack at only fifty-nine years of age, leaving her to support herself and her fifteen-year-old daughter.

Alice feels that age is an advantage in childrearing; it brings wisdom.

"I think my parents were both wise. I also wonder whether or not adults who've had a chance to be alone and meet some of their own needs and to spend those years pleasuring themselves, when they have children, does it seem less of a sacrifice? Do they feel they are ready for the demands? I certainly felt that. I felt I had wonderful years being childless, in which I traveled to Europe extensively. I had a chance to work and have a sense of my own talents and abilities. By the time I had children, I had no trouble leaving work. I was ready for this transition, ready to develop my skills in another area."

"That isn't necessarily happening today, though," I replied, "Young women are developing careers before they have children and then fitting babies into their careers. They aren't giving up their careers but continuing them, and adding children."

"I'm not in favor of that!" Alice said, her tone brisk. "That's not something I'm in favor of. Certainly not in the beginning. I feel very strongly that children in the early years of life need to bond with the mother. And women who have children and then turn them over to day care centers at six months or eight months of age, I think they're doing something very destructive and I don't see how these children can help but grow up with some scars from this. I very much wanted my children when I had them; I loved being home with them. As you know, I've gone back to school now. I don't feel I've made my children my life or that I've had them in order to fulfill all my reasons for being, but I think there's a correct time, and my children . . . " She broke off, laughing. "This is terribly biased . . . I see them as very independent. Very secure." She paused for a moment and began again.

"I asked my children last night—I told them you were coming to talk to me about being the child of an older mother, and they jokingly said, 'Well, *we* have an older mother.' And I said, 'Am I much older than the mothers of your friends?' And they pointed out that I was, indeed. I asked them if it meant anything to them and my daughter, who's more verbal than my son, did say that she thought her parents would die before the parents of her friends and that when some of her friends asked her the ages of her parents, she would often get a shocked response when she'd tell them her father is fifty-four. . . . Even so, while my daughter did express this thought, I don't see it as something she worries about a great deal."

"Well, it's something you can reassure her about, simply by pointing to grandma!" I said.

"Of course! And that's exactly what I said, and I shared with her that I'd had that thought growing up as well, and that I understood it . . . . Of course, we never know . . . "

"Yes," I agreed. "That's the point. Even young parents can die in a car crash . . . "

"Absolutely! There are no guarantees."

Alice went on to discuss her husband's involvement with their children's lives, to emphasize the importance of parents, especially older parents, participating in their children's activities.

"From the time our son was little, my husband has gone to all the soccer games . . . yet I know of younger parents who don't come to the games. They drop the kids off and they pick 'em up. These are the things, I think, that make a difference to children. But, especially, you must give children a sense of independence, a strong sense of their abilities. If you create that environment, the children will be able to cope, whatever happens."

Alice also feels that children should be born close together so they can share each other, have each other to turn to and to lean upon.

Janet Spruce, adopted when her mother was forty, her father forty-seven, does not plan to wait longer than her late twenties to have children. She feels somewhat trapped, limited, by her parents' age, especially by her father's ill health, and by the expectation that she will not leave home, except to marry. Her older brother and her younger sister have left their parents' home, leaving Janet, she feels, to carry the burden.

"My Dad has diabetes—he's had that for about five years. He was in the hospital two years ago and he has leukemia, too, which is in remission right now. He really doesn't do much." Her voice became thin, her throat contracting as she tried to hold back her tears, "He just kind of sits and eats and watches TV. He isn't active at all. He should take walks but he doesn't do it."

Janet finds it difficult, under these circumstances, to leave and, in part, does not want to leave her parents.

"They don't want to be left alone. They feel older . . . and they want someone there with them. They just don't want to be left alone."

One reason for wanting to have children earlier than her mother did, she said, is that she wants to be energetic with her children. "My mother got tired . . . . And when people get older they become a bit more nervous. When they're younger, they can tolerate more. At least, that's how it was with my Mom."

Stephen Grey, an only child who grew up in a single parent household was so lonely and unhappy as a child that he is adamant in condemning his "pattern" of family life. He feels that a woman, regardless of age, should not have children unless she has a husband to share in the rearing.

"A child needs a father . . . at least, that was my experience. Nothing can substitute for a father . . . a boy needs a male model."

Of all the now adult late-born children questioned for this study, less than one-fourth recommend late parenting. One of these, though, Charles Finch, in his late thirties and single, while enthusiastic that others delay childbearing and child-rearing until they are financially and emotionally settled, claims he will not have children himself, even if he marries.

Peter Cochran considers his childhood was enhanced by his older parents' patience and devotion to him but the major reason for favoring late parenting for himself, as it is for Meg Perkins and Frank Martin, is to allow time to develop his career, untrammeled by domestic responsibilities.

Alice Marshall has chosen relatively late-parenting for herself, her children being the products of her second marriage, and feels that age is an advantage in childrearing. Her parents, she says, were wise and she, too, acquired wisdom and a sense of self in the thirty-four years before she became a parent. When a woman is ready to start a family, though, the children should take priority over all other activities, Alice feels, especially in their early years of life. Later, the woman can resume her career, or her studies, but a small child needs a mother, not a day care center.

While those children of older parents who had been relatively happy as children were more likely to choose late parenting for themselves, or to recommend it to others, than those who perceived themselves as having been unhappy as children, even some of those preferred not to see the pattern repeated.

Marilyn Henry had not intended to follow in her mother's footsteps and now regrets her ten-year wait to start a family, that regret having much to do with recognition in her own child of worries that concerned her when she was young: "Is Mommy going to die before I'm grown up?" and "Who will take care of me if that happens?"

Jim Compton, though happy as the child of older parents, has been determined, "for as long as I can remember," he says, to have his children while he is still young. Jim, now understanding his older father's inability to be athletically active, "to play ball with the lads," wants his children to know him, and remember him, as physically strong, as not yet in decline.

Few of the offspring of older parents who were unhappy as children either want children late in their own lives or would recommend others to have late-born children. Some of those still unmarried and childless, though, as they approach and reach their thirties, admit that this may, of necessity, be the pattern they follow.

Cheryl Greenham says she does not want to be denied the experience of having a child or children, and has thought, fleetingly, of having a baby and rearing it on her own, should she not find a suitable man to marry. She is not alone in this yearning for children as the years pass. According to *Ms* magazine, in the age range of twenty-five to thirty-nine years, unmarried women are the fastest growing category of women giving birth. Cheryl's years in the classroom, though, have shown her that children of single mothers appear to have problems other children do not face. Stephen Grey, who feels keenly the lack of a father in his young life, also agrees that children need two parents. He attributes his unhappiness as a child more to having no father than to being the child of an older mother.

The "testimony" of the late-born children in this study does not demonstrate overwhelming advocacy of late-parenting. From the children's standpoint, while older parents may have more patience and, perhaps, more money, than younger parents, the disadvantages of being born late in their parents' lives outweigh the advantages. Most would not choose older parenting for themselves or recommend it for others and many voiced strong objections to the trend.

7

The Late-Born Child:
Advantages and
Disadvantages

When you're older, you're wiser—Charles Finch

My parents were always tired when I was young—Margaret Pearce

More babies are born to women aged twenty to twenty-four years than to any other group in this country. Since the 1970s, and continuing into the eighties, however, significantly large numbers of women have chosen, and are choosing, to delay childbearing until their thirties and even until their forties. As Landon Jones points out in *Great Expectations,* the birthrate in 1970 for women aged thirty to thirty-four having a first baby was 7.3 per thousand. In 1977, as the baby boomers reached that age bracket, the rate rose 36 percent to 9.9 per thousand. Jones lists several well-known women, such as Erica Jong, Paula Prentiss, and Nora Ephron, who had their first babies in their mid-thirties. Nora Ephron, in her *New York Times Magazine* article wrote, "Just once in my life, I would like to do something everyone else is not doing, but that seems not to be my destiny." Nor, adds Landon Jones, will it be the destiny for the 37 million baby-boom women who will face a similar moment of decision.

This study of twenty-two men and women who were born to older-than-average parents is an attempt to learn how those now-adult late-born children felt about their older parents, and how they feel now about late-parenting. The reminiscences, the remembered pains, and the remembered pleasures, while unique in some ways, given the varied circumstances of the families into which the children were born and the different personalities of their parents, also yield patterns shared by many of those interviewed.

Those patterns, those recurring statements and themes emerging from the interviews, provide insights that may be useful to those contemplating late childbearing. Instead of looking at the late-born child from the parents' viewpoint: How would this child enhance our lives? How would a baby affect our relationship to each other? What effect will a baby have on my career?—reasonable questions that should be addressed— this study asks the *children* of older parents about their childhood experiences and how they feel their lives have been affected by them.

This study did not begin with a hypothesis, as do many scientific studies; no prior assumptions were made about what would, or would not, be found. Instead, the research questions were generated after several open-ended interviews probing the advantages and disadvantages of being a late-born child had been taped and transcribed and certain common themes were discerned in the stories the subjects told. About half those interviewed appeared to have been reasonably happy as children, hardly aware that their parents were older than the parents of their same-age friends or, if they were aware of it, their parents' age was not cause for particular concern. Indeed, for some of this group, their parents' age was seen as advantageous. The rest of the subjects, though, were keenly conscious as children that their parents were older than most of their schoolmates' parents, and they felt their childhood years had been profoundly and significantly discolored by this fact.

Questions

Guiding questions for this study then became, What makes the difference in childhood happiness among late-born children? Given that many couples are choosing to delay parenting, what might they do to assure that their age has the least negative impact on their children? What steps can older parents take to help their children lead relatively happy, untroubled lives?

To help answer these questions, several others were posed: Do *only* children of older parents feel especially disadvantaged or, rather, especially advantaged, compared to children who have to share resources with their brothers and sisters? How does the "caboose" baby fare, the child born after (sometimes long after) his or her siblings? Do children perceive that parents in their fifties, even their sixties, remember and understand the turmoil of adolescence as well as younger parents do? Do children of older parents feel especially driven to achieve? Do children of older parents feel they face problems that seem to be unique to them? Are children embarrassed by parents much older than the parents of their friends? Do late-born children have special worries about their parents' deaths? Can this study show anything about children of *single* older parents? Can the perceived advantages and disadvantages of being born to older parents be distinguished and classified? and What do late-born children think can be done by older parents to ensure reasonably secure and happy childhood years for their offspring?

Answers

Does the Only Child of Older Parents Feel Especially Advantaged or Disadvantaged?

Seven of the twenty-two late-born children interviewed for

this study were only children. All felt lonely at times, they said, and all regretted to some extent the lack of brothers and sisters when they were growing up. The two only children of *single* parents expressed particularly strong negative feelings about their childhood years.

Brothers and sisters, as every one who has them knows, can be nuisances. They grab the last slice of cake on the plate and stuff it in their mouths too swiftly for the one deprived to do more than protest. If they are older or bigger, they give orders and push the younger, smaller children around. Siblings are not unmixed blessings. But the child who grows up with other children has built-in companions, adored or not. An older brother or sister can be turned to for explanations and solutions for problems that one is loath to take to Mom or Dad. A younger sister or brother can make a child feel protective at times, powerful, intelligent, and knowing. And while a child may not always be in harmony with a brother or a sister, an only child must always look for friends and companions outside the home. Those successful in making friends appear to have missed siblings less than those whose outside social contacts were limited.

For Peter Cochran, his parents were his closest friends, paying considerable attention to the child's interests and intellectual needs, spending most of their time away from work with him. Peter appeared to feel his parents' devotion to him compensated for his lack of siblings, but he also saw it as limiting in some ways, narrowing the range of ways of seeing the world and responding to its challenges.

Children seem to need other children if they are to be children themselves and to feel comfortable acting in childish ways. Several of the only children in the sample spoke of having been too old for their age, of being little adults, of never having been children, and some spoke of not having much empathy for little children, even now. Only children who find, or are provided with, substitutes for siblings: cousins or friends, or, if no young people are available, grandparents or surrogate grandparents, express fewer regrets about their childhood years than do those whose social circle was narrower.

While Peter Cochran expressed satisfaction with his childhood as the only child of older parents, seeing the devotion to him by his parents as an advantage he seemed to think was unavailable to children of younger parents, few of the only children of older parents interviewed perceived themselves as especially advantaged or, in any way, compensated for the lack of siblings. Marilyn Henry, whose mother had died less than a year before she was interviewed, was feeling anew pangs of regret over her lack of siblings. "When my father dies," she said, "there will be *no one else.*" There would be no one with whom to share the memories of childhood, to say "remember when?" "Even if it's a brother or sister you hate" Marilyn added, leaving the rest of the sentence hanging in the air.

What about only children of single parents?

The only children of single older parents in the sample left little doubt about their feelings of having been deeply disadvantaged.

Jean Smythe remembers her childhood and adolescent years as profoundly troubled and sees her troubles as stemming directly from her lack of a father and from her lack of siblings. As a tiny child, exceptionally early, according to the psychological literature, her concern that her mother might die, leaving her with no one to care for her, became, at times, obsessive. "I was terrified of being left alone." She knew, also early in her life, that her mother was old. Her only other relative, a grandmother who was about seventy years older than Jean, Jean perceived as *really* old. "If there had been two parents . . . siblings" Jean said, still wistful about what she felt she had missed.

Jean's loneliness and her fears of being left totally alone may have been prompted, or reinforced, by her isolation from other children. She met few other children before she started school and found her first few days there "crushing," not knowing how other children behaved or how she should respond to them.

She describes her need for a family as "desperate." If her mother would not, or could not, provide her with brothers and sisters, she would have to make them for herself. She became sexually active in her early teens, deliberately trying to become pregnant and was frustrated when she did not conceive. Afraid she might be barren, she studied ways to promote fertility, spending hours searching the literature in the medical library and turning to a gynecologist for advice.

Jean married at sixteen, an unsuitable match, as it turned out, ending in divorce but giving her the two children—"the brother and sister I never had"—she so desperately wanted.

Stephen Grey, whose father died when Stephen was three years old (too early for the child to remember him) recalls his childhood and adolescence without joy, as years of loneliness with few people to lean upon for emotional support. He perceived his mother as having withdrawn from him into her own world of books, not recognizing his need for attention, especially his need for help with his reading. Of far more importance to him than his mother's age was the void he felt in his life because he lacked a father and because he had no brother or sister. "She could adopt one!" he blurted during our interview. Until then, his responses had been cautious, taciturn, but a question about his lack of siblings seemed to touch him deeply, transporting this man of, now, forty years, back to his early childhood and the pain he felt then.

While neither Jean Smythe's story, nor that of Stephen Grey, may be typical or representative of the experience of all, or most, only children of single older parents, they are pertinent. According to Robin Warshaw, in a recent issue of *Ms* Magazine, unmarried women aged twenty-five to thirty-nine are the fastest growing category of women giving birth. For several reasons, including that as women grow older, particularly as they pass thirty years of age, the pool of men eligible as husbands decreases, increasing numbers of women are choosing to bear children without being married. Dr. Patricia Conrad, a Manhattan gynecologist, cited in the *New York Times*, counsels women who are beyond traditional childbearing years and who may, therefore, be at some medical risk. Conrad describes her typical unmarried patient as a career-oriented woman aged thirty-five to forty-two years. "That's when they hit the panic button," she explains. The older single patient who consciously chooses pregnancy was rare even as recently as the mid 1970s but "I'm seeing this all the time now," the doctor said. Some women, rather than risk legal problems and demands from the fathers of their children, are choosing artificial insemination.

These older single mothers are more likely to consider their families complete with one child than to have two or more children. On a Phil Donahue program aired in Los Angeles in September 1984, a single mother in her thirties said, "I just wanted a baby." Another, thirty-seven years old when her baby was born, confirmed, "I wanted to be a mother." And Jane Mattes, a psychotherapist, quoted by Judy Klemesrud in the *New York Times*, realizing that, perhaps, Mr. Right was not going to come along after all, decided to have a child outside marriage when she was thirty-six years old. "The biological time-clock was ticking ... and the idea of life without a child was unthinkable to me. Having a child was part of my value system, because life without intimacy doesn't allow you to grow." Having fulfilled what these single women feel is a biological and emotional need by having a baby, added children might seem just too great a burden, given the pressing demands of a career. Her job becomes even more important to the single woman, when the support of a child rests solely with her. And, as Sharon Lovick, who runs a center for teenage mothers, points out: babies don't give, they take. A baby brings responsibilities and constant demands, as well as some joys, to its mother, no matter what her age.

The childhood experiences of Jean Smythe and Stephen

Grey may have been especially trying and hard, but they do offer some hints about the more obvious pitfalls that single parents might avoid in their childrearing. If a child has neither father nor siblings, ways can be found to fill the void, provide substitutes. Rather than sheltering the child from the outside world, as did Jean's mother, or leaving him to struggle alone with his perceived inadequacies, as did Stephen's mother, parenting an only child seems to require a special perceptiveness, an even sharper awareness of needs than does parenting a child who is part of a larger family. On the one hand, it may require a willingness to let go, to share the child with others and allow the child exposure to the influence of those others. But the fine line between "allowing the child exposure to the influence of others" and abandoning him or her may not always be clear to the child for, on the other hand, single parenting requires extra giving of one's self. Children need to know they are loved and that they are important to their parents and that their parents will be available when they are needed; they need to feel protected—but not stifled.

While time is one the scarcest commodities available to working parents, participation in activities that help their children broaden their circle of friends of all ages appears to be helpful in eliminating children's feelings of being alone. Attending PTA meetings and other school functions allows families to interact with other families and helps create and reinforce friendships among the children. Social activities centered around church or temple may aid only children in developing a feeling of belonging to a group, of having others in the community who are, in a sense, family members, substitute siblings and substitute parents, as may family participation in the activities of hobby clubs and associations or fitness and sports groups.

How does the "caboose" baby fare?

Eleven of the late-born children interviewed for this study were "caboose" babies, born several years after other siblings.

The age gap between these children and their brother or sister closest in age ranged from about five years to thirteen years. The gap between the caboose babies and their oldest sibling ranged from ten to twenty years. One caboose baby, Sylvia Shaw, was really one of a pair of caboose babies, born only two and a half years apart; an older pair of sisters, however, were ten and thirteen years older than Sylvia.

The caboose baby might once have been the issue of its mother's menopause, born long after the parents thought further procreation was possible and no longer practiced birth control. The "menopause baby" is still a possibility of course, but, with the increase in divorce and remarriage in the last two decades, the late-born baby may be the choice of couples previously married to other partners, with children from those unions, who want a child of this new alliance while there is still time.

One of the now-grown caboose babies interviewed, Margaret Pearce, spoke of her older parents and of her position in the family as latecomer with sadness and some anger. Her resentments were several and enduring. Her parents, she felt, were old-fashioned; they were preoccupied with their work to the extent of abandoning their parental responsibilities for her to their other daughter, ten years older than Margaret. Their desire to take their youngest child on picnics or to museums or to participate in her activities had been eroded by having already done those things with their older children, and any interest they may have had in small children was diverted from Margaret to their grandchild, the child of Margaret's brother, the first-born in the family, seventeen years older than Margaret. Further, her mother, Margaret felt, had little understanding of her needs; such attention as her mother paid to the girl, like shopping with her for new clothes, was, in Margaret's view, misguided. The unsuitable, if expensive, garments she chose for the girl only added to Margaret's feeling that she was different from other children her age.

While she loved and depended upon her sister, ten years

older than she, who was given responsibility for Margaret's care, her relationship with her much older brother was virtually non-existent. The boy left home for college soon after Margaret was born and the two never knew each other or became close. Even now, at forty years of age, and with children of her own, her sadness over the "loss" of her brother still grieves her, still brings tears brimming over. The two now relate as distant acquaintances: "We pass polite conversation, just as you would with a stranger." The distance is geographical as well as emotional, Margaret living on the West Coast, her brother living in the east.

If Margaret remembers her childhood with regret, her feelings, now, about her parents are even more painful. Her mother and father, who live on the East Coast, close to her brother, are both ill. Their great age, Margaret feels, repercusses on her children now, as it did on her when she was younger. Her children cannot know or enjoy their grandparents, as do their friends. Grandma and Grandpa cannot take vacations with them, cannot be relied upon to "sit" with the children while Margaret and her husband go away for a weekend on their own, as can the parents of Margaret's same-age friends. And, repeating the pattern of the past, she feels her own children are as separated from their cousins by age as she was from her sister and brother.

Most other caboose babies' memories of their childhood were not as bitter as were those of Margaret Pearce, nor of Barbara Anderson, who found her older sister's attentions to her own small daughter made Barbara's lack of attention from her mother even more apparent. Indeed, for Charles Finch, his sister, older than he by thirteen years, was like a concerned, considerate, dear friend as well as a second, younger mother. He feels, as do Alice Marshall, Jim Compton, and Christine Strongman, that having a substantially older sister was comforting. And Margaret Pearce, despite the unhappiness she feels at the distance between herself and her much older brother, acknowledges her appreciation of, and love for, the sister who served her as second mother. Ted Martelli, too, although having many reservations about being the last child of elderly parents, appreciated the part his middle sister played in his upbringing. Still, Ted does not remember finding much other comfort in his sisters, who were so much older than he. As the only boy in a houseful of young women, he felt, he said, isolated among his adult siblings, especially as he was discouraged by his mother, "who was finicky about her house," from bringing friends home.

The remaining caboose babies, however, spoke of their older brothers and sisters, sometimes one sibling in particular, with pleasure and appreciation. Even though separated by years and geography from her older brothers, simply knowing they would take care of her should she need them, gave Alice Marshall a feeling of security. Her mother asked for, and received, assurance from her older son, nearly nine years older than Alice, that he would take responsibility for the girl, should that ever be necessary. In turn, she was able to give that assurance to her daughter.

Jim Compton hardly knew his brothers, sixteen and nineteen years his senior, and still feels distant from them, but his sister, ten years older than he, provided companionship, friendship, and, ultimately, a younger "brother" for Jim, by marrying very young and having her first baby when Jim was eight years old.

The differences between the perceptions of their childhood years of Margaret Pearce and Jim Compton are remarkable, given substantial similarities in their circumstances. Margaret's parents were both forty-two years old when she was born; Jim's mother was forty, his father forty-four, at Jim's birth. Both sets of parents held full-time jobs and relied upon a daughter to take care of their youngest child. Jim hardly knew his older brothers; Margaret, too, felt her brother was like a stranger. Jim became an uncle, Margaret became an aunt, when each was eight years of age. Yet Margaret perceives her childhood years as marred in many ways, and feels her life is still affected by her experiences then; Jim sees his childhood years as happy and is contented, now, with his family life.

When one looks closer at the differences in the parents' attitudes toward their respective caboose babies, as those attitudes are perceived by those children, it may be possible to account for some of the differences in the now-adult children's feelings about their early years. Margaret's parents were tired of participating in their children's activities. They hardly ever involved themselves in anything that interested their youngest child: "They were involved in other things by then," Margaret said. If Margaret went to ball games or to club events, she was taken, not by her mother and father, but by her friends' parents. Jim's mother and father, by contrast, spent all their spare time with Jim and his sister: "on the weekends, we'd all go someplace. We were always doing something." And Jim, keen on baseball, could rely upon his parents to come and watch any game in which he played: "They were always there and they were always supportive of whatever I did . . . they'd go to Open House . . . they were just involved in what I was doing. And at home, we'd always play Scrabble or Monopoly or things like that, and card games. Card games were our big thing."

Margaret resented her brother's child, seeing this new baby as a competitor for her parents' affection and interest. Jim, though, was made to feel important as an uncle, as someone who could teach things to the new baby, someone to whom he could play a caring older "brother." Jim's nephew enhanced Jim's childhood; her brother's child seemed to Margaret to draw down the small stock of attention her mother and father could spare for her.

It is not the intention here to pass judgment on the parents of the interviewees but, rather, to learn from what appear to have been their strengths and weaknesses in childrearing. Caboose babies can be advantaged in some ways, compared to children whose siblings are close to them in age. They can benefit from having older siblings, can gain an extra sense of comfort from having two "mothers," one young, one substantially older, and can feel affection and appreciation for much older siblings who, even though long gone from the home and little more than strangers, can serve in some ways as sources of security.

The stories told by the caboose babies, like those of only late-born children, indicate that they are happier when they feel themselves loved and wanted, when their parents spend time with them and share some of their interests, and that the older sibling, or siblings, can provide extra, near-adult companionship, as did Charles Finch's sister and Jim Compton's sister, to augment that of attentive parents. And even if the parents are too busy, or too tired, to devote much of themselves to the child, older brothers and sisters can be turned to for attention, care, and advice. This was the experience of Christine Strongman, whose older sisters watched over her and, ultimately, included her as a performer on their show-business tours. Unlike the only child, the caboose baby with a brother or sister still at home, does not always have to go searching for someone to talk to.

Do older parents remember and understand the turmoil of adolescence?

Many youngsters, feeling that their parents grew up in the Dark Ages, claim it is impossible for Mom and Dad to understand contemporary teenagers, to remember what it feels like to be in love, or to experience the insistent sexual urges that make it difficult to think about humdrum activities like studying or taking out the garbage. If this is true for adolescents whose parents are only one generation removed from them, how do those youngsters feel who are separated from their mothers and fathers by a double generation gap?

As a youngster, Margaret Pearce couldn't believe that her parents remembered anything about sex. They seemed very old, she said, to have produced her at over forty years of age.

"That was something I could never understand. How could they have done that when they were so *old!*" Margaret felt she could not turn to her mother when she needed someone to confide in. Like some other caboose babies, she was told "the facts of life" by her older sister.

Sylvia Shaw, a late-born child with much older sisters as well as a sister born only two-and-a-half years before she was, sees her parents as being out of date in their childrearing practices but, like several other caboose babies, her two older sisters were there to confide in and to share with her all the latest fads and fashions. Janet Spruce, too, is grateful she had her sister as confidante. "We talked all the time. If I didn't have her, I don't know what I would have done.... There was no way I could talk to my Mom. I still can't, to this day... she doesn't understand my generation."

The only child, though, has no siblings to ask for information or advice about sex or any other subject. Stephen Grey, a lonely, only child, feels his mother never really understood his needs at all, either when he was a child or as an adolescent, and that she should have perceived his longing for help and attention. He felt he had nowhere to turn for any kind of advice or comfort, no outlet for emotion, and that, rather than trying to find out and encourage those pursuits that interested him, his mother pressed him to follow in his dead father's professional footsteps.

Cheryl Greenham, born of her father's second marriage, saw her father's years as a decided obstacle to his understanding of her as a girl. She remembers how hurt she felt when he failed to say how pretty she looked, even though he had complimented her friend. "He didn't understand what it was to be a young woman. He was so old!"

Peter Cochran, who sees his childhood as happy and his parents as devoted and caring, felt close to his mother and father and able to discuss almost any subject with them. He did have some reservations, though, about their understanding of him as a teenager. His mother, a trained nurse, had taught him about the mechanics of sex but he felt his parents lacked understanding of "the problems of a teenage boy trying desperately to express himself as a sexual being . . . because they were a little out of touch with those feelings. Forty years is a long time! You tend to forget some of the details and some of the pain of that." Peter feels his friend's younger parents were able to deal with their children's sexuality better than his own parents did.

Rosemary Cross, also an only child, felt the age gap between her mother and herself most keenly when she entered her teens and young womanhood. Her mother was years behind the younger parents of her friends in allowing the girl to wear make-up or to discard her hated long knee socks for nylon stockings. "I had no role model," she added. Her mother's style of dressing was staid and matronly. "It was not what I wanted to copy." On the other hand, Priscilla Banks expressed amusement, rather than sorrow, when she spoke of her mother's clothes as frumpy and matronly, compared to the clothes worn by her friends' younger mothers. Priscilla's memories of her childhood and adolescence are warm. She and her mother were always able to talk together and, in her forties, Priscilla says her relationship with her mother, in her seventies, remains loving and caring.

Ted Martelli regrets his lack of closeness to his father. He remembers having few people to confide in at any stage in his childhood and youth. His father spent little time with him, the only son, even after he retired. "I guess it was just that . . . he was so distant in age from me so he couldn't have much in common with me." And Rebecca Johnson, whose mother was only thirty-one at Rebecca's birth, regrets the lack of closeness to her mother. "She always seemed old . . . . She wasn't a companion, or like an older girl friend, like the relationship some of the girls [her friends] had with their mothers. And I do feel that had to do with the age difference." Jim Compton, too, says he talked to friends, teachers, and basketball coaches when he had problems as a teenager. He did not speak to his parents, he says, "because they had a different understanding from what I think I wanted to hear. And because of the era that they came from, they had different thinking." Now, though, at twenty years of age, Jim feels able to be more open with his parents because they see things as he does.

From the stories told in this study, the double generation gap between older parents and their adolescent children seemed significant for some, less significant for others, and of no significance for a few. Most of those who examine generational differences would probably agree that the emotions expressed by these children of older parents are not markedly different from those that might be voiced by adolescent children of parents of any age. Some parents find it easier to discuss personal and emotional matters with their children than do others, just as some adolescents are more able to confide in their parents than are others. Some late-born children perceived their parents as too old to remember the passions of youth, but the same could probably be said of many children born to younger parents.

For youngsters, including caboose babies, who feel they cannot confide in their parents, but who have older brothers or sisters still at home, the problems of growing up appear to be more easily aired and shared than are those for only children or for those whose siblings have grown up and gone away. Margaret Pearce, Sylvia Shaw, Janet Spruce, and Christine Strongman all had receptive older sisters. But only children again seem to be disadvantaged unless they have friends or can find adults they can trust. Stephen Grey had no one in whom to confide. His bitter, "I talked . . . to a tree!" indicates his frustration as a boy and as an adolescent. Peter Cochran, another only child, although close to his parents in many ways, felt the age difference between them most keenly in his early teens; he felt his parents were out of touch, compared to the younger parents of his friends. And even though Rebecca Johnson had a brother, he was younger than she and, thus, unable to serve as adviser. She found it impossible to speak of intimate things with her mother and, it seems, with outsiders. She remains, she says, shy about sharing personal matters with anyone. Some in the study, though, were able to find teachers and other school personnel to serve as sounding boards for their ideas or as advisers on personal subjects.

As has been seen repeatedly in these brief summaries of specific themes, when children of older parents, especially those with few close family members, can widen their social circles to include friends and acquaintances of a range of ages, they seem able to cope more easily at each stage of growing up.

Do children of older parents feel especially driven to achieve?

Despite some experts' contentions that older parents may have especially high expectations of their children and exert burdensome pressure upon them, the evidence from this study does not indicate that these children of older parents felt especially driven to achieve. Exceptions to this were Stephen Grey, Peter Cochran, and Meg Perkins, all only children.

The pressure Stephen Grey's mother put on him to achieve—and to achieve in the same way as did his deceased father—was, he felt, oppressive. He was not interested in becoming a lawyer, but he conformed to his mother's wishes by taking pre-law classes in college and by attending law school. After one year, he dropped out of graduate school, at last expressing his long-suppressed distaste for the subjects he was studying. He drifted from one lowly job to another until finally entering a field in which he felt comfortable. Only recently, at forty years of age, has he begun to establish himself as a professional.

Peter Cochran says he doesn't remember his parents ever speaking openly of their expectation that he would perform well; they did not need to. Peter has always driven himself, but he sees his parents' wishes for him to excel as implicit in their actions. "They were extremely subtle," he said. They demonstrated their expectations in the things they did and the ways they did them. His mother, a career professional, was committed both to her career and to rearing her child. Peter sees her as "driven," perceiving, and regretting—to some extent—the same trait in himself. "I'm very aware of catching myself weighing certain things very highly. Demanding a lot of myself. Demanding a great deal of success, achievement ... and knowing that's something I have to be aware of and temper." He added that he would try, at least for a while after leaving college, "to let things take their course instead of constantly watching and checking." His parents, he admitted, had been his most important role models, "successful in setting things up and doing things very well and demanding a lot out of themselves."

As a child, Meg Perkins felt unsure about her ability to meet her father's high expectations of her. "They [her parents] figured out when I was a very young age that I was 'brilliant.' " She laughed before continuing. "I had perfect pitch and all these wonderful talents ... they *did* have very high expectations, especially my Dad ... piano lessons ... and singing." Meg adored her father and perceived him as playful and youthful. He died at sixty-five, when Meg was thirteen, leaving her, she said, "devastated ... for years to come.... That kind of affected me for a long time." Her father, she says, idolized her, which may have been a factor in her lack of self-confidence as a child. "I think it had to do with my Dad having ... you know, living up to his expectations of me ... What I should be doing. What I should be able to do ... Being a wonder kid for my Dad ... I just remember being worried about it. You know, am I ... *enough?* ... Having doubts whether what he kept *telling* me I was, *was* what I was." Even now, at twenty-five, and twelve years after father's death, she still confesses to those same doubts.

Other late-born children, though, did not feel they had been under any special pressure to succeed or, if achievement was emphasized, as for Charles Finch and his much older sister, it seemed a reasonable expectation, given their upper middle-class background. Rosemary Cross, too, whose father had attended university, took it for granted that she would follow his example. "But, on the other hand, they [her parents] always said, 'If you don't do well, we'll still love you. We'll just figure out something else to do.' " And Sylvia Shaw, the last-born of four girls, felt any pressure to succeed came from herself and from school. "Mother didn't expect *anything* of the two youngest. She leaned on the older girls harder. She says she was too tired when the younger girls came along." One young man, Frank Martin, regretted his parents' lack of interest in his educational achievements. "I might do a lot better than I'm doing now if I had pressure on me, if they were a bit more encouraging."

The number of children of older parents in this study who felt pressured to achieve is small, but it can be noted that those who were aware of such pressure were only children. It is possible that the only child, regardless of his or her parents' ages, may feel he or she must bear more responsibility for fulfilling parental dreams than does the child with brothers and sisters.

Are late-born children embarrassed by their older parents?

With few exceptions, the children of older parents interviewed for this study were aware that their parents were older than the parents of their classmates and either were embarrassed by it or felt a sense of sadness and shame for their parents.

"She was so much older . . . she looked different from the other mothers . . . and I was embarrassed, ashamed to have her come to school and pick me up. . . . I wouldn't introduce her to my friends if I could help it" said Christine Strongman.

Most of the interviewees spoke of times when their parents were mistaken for their grandparents and most found this experience upsetting:

"People used to say things like, 'Your grandpa's here to pick you up' or 'your grandma,' and they would laugh when they found out it was my parents," said Jim Compton of his mother and father. "But I didn't think it was funny. I didn't like that. It seemed they were making fun of them. . . . I didn't want people to think that they were old."

"People would ask if those were my grandparents and I would *die* of embarrassment. I mean, when you're a child, you want to be like your peers and it's sort of hard to handle," said Cheryl Greenham.

Jean Smythe felt more sadness than embarrassment when her mother was mistaken for her grandmother, her sadness stemming both from her mother's years and from her mother's inability to talk to her about her age, keeping it a "secret," she thought, until the child was thirteen years old. Jean, though, had known how old her mother was since her fifth or sixth year and was made anxious by her mother's unwillingness to acknowledge the reality of her years.

Rebecca Johnson's mother always seemed old to Rebecca, older than the mothers of her friends. Her mother, divorced and totally responsible for the well-being of her two children, was often tired—not a lively companion to her daughter, as Rebecca perceived her friends' mothers were to them.

And Margaret Pearce remembers feeling resentful when people referred to her mother as her grandmother. "I got furious! And I said 'This is my *mother!*' "

Our society appears to be obsessed with youth and with remaining youthful, an obsession constantly fed by manufacturers, whose profits are predicated on our yearning to be forever young, and by plastic surgeons whose practices flourish as more and more people are persuaded to have the evidence of the years sliced from their faces. Even eighty-year-olds are succumbing to societal strictures against growing old gracefully!

According to an article in the *Los Angeles Times* of February 17, 1985:

People in their 60s, 70s, and 80s who in the past accepted wrinkled faces are now seeking surgical improvement in ever-increasing numbers. Even younger people are seeking plastic surgery. Some feel the procedure restores a youthful image and helps them compete in the market place.

Our television programs are interrupted by advertisements for creams alleged to minimize "the tiny lines and wrinkles" that make us look old, and magazines, too, including *Ms.*, which appeals, supposedly, to a more enlightened and "liberated" audience than do many other women's publications, carry advertisements warning that when skin slows down, "the top layers stay on too long. Look dull. Old."

"Old" is an ugly word in our culture, a word used by skillful copywriters to encourage us to regard skin not as an organ that contains and protects the underlying tissues but as a facade that must, itself, be protected, pampered, and preserved to remain as it was when we were infants. No sign of life's experiences, hardships, and joys must be discerned on its surface. Our hair, too, must never reveal our age and we must struggle to keep our bodies as youthful, slim, and lithe as they never were when we were in our teens!

It is not surprising that many children of older parents, who imbibe cultural expectations, values, and beliefs with their baby formula, feel embarrassed and sad when their parents do not fit the image of youth held out for people of all ages in our society. These feelings may be exacerbated when the parents, who have also absorbed society's views about aging and made them their own, hide their age, or lie about it, as though it were shameful. On the other hand, older parents who are comfortable about their age, who take it for granted and speak of it freely, may help their children, too, to accept it without anxiety or concern, recognizing that "youthful appearance" is only superficial window dressing, hardly to be compared with the many important and enduring virtues for which people can be loved and respected.

Do children of older parents feel they have unique problems?

Several interviewees for this study had long been aware of their special problems as children of older parents, but even those whose childhood years were not adversely affected by their parents' ages were becoming aware in their young or middle adulthood of responsibilities that would not concern their contemporaries with younger parents.

It is true that death can strike at any age. The speeding car, the derailed train, accidents of all kinds, kill without regard to years. But the child with parents clearly much older than the parents of his or her age-mates may have special fears about parental loss. Even given current normal life expectancies, late-born children are more likely to lose a parent, especially a father, through natural causes than are children of younger parents.

Meg Perkins and Alice Marshall both lost their fathers when they were teenagers. Meg's father died of cancer at sixty-five—a little short of his expected life span—when Meg was thirteen, and Alice's father died of a heart attack at the age of fifty-nine, when Alice was fifteen. Despite substantial improvement in the prevention and treatment of heart conditions, heart disease is still the major killer of men in their middle years. A man who delays fatherhood until his late thirties, forties, or fifties, is not as likely to see his children reach adulthood as is one whose children are born in his twenties or early thirties. Children of older parents are aware of this and worry about it. Frank Martin, at seventeen, is concerned that one or both of his parents might die before he finishes college. And Celia Abbott, an otherwise happy and cheerful high-schooler, expressed her fear that "my parents will die before I'm an adult."

But even if, as is likely, both parents survive to live long, the late-born child may confront responsibilities that those with younger parents will be spared until much later in their lives. The vast majority of people remain fit and active as they age.

Certainly, through their sixties, and even into their seventies, most men and women still feel as though they are "young," if not as young as they "used to be." It is in the mid-seventies, according to Robert Binstock, director of the Policy Center on Aging at the Heller School for Advanced Studies in Social Welfare, when the risk of disabling disease is the greatest. And, when their parents are in their mid-seventies, late-born children may still be in their twenties and thirties.

Charles Finch, a happy child and a well-adjusted adolescent deeply appreciative of his parents' affection and support, began to see in his thirties that his mother and father were growing older and more infirm. Each time he visited them in their home state, about twice a year, they seemed, he said, to have aged noticeably more. Now, Charles' father, in his early eighties, has become "forgetful" and in need of constant surveillance, his mother has been seriously ill with cancer, and Charles, in an attempt to keep his parents together for as long as possible, is making plans, at considerable disruption to his career, to either move near them or to have them move to where he lives.

Cheryl Greenham, at thirty, has already nursed her father through his final, long illness. Cheryl felt keenly the pull of responsibility to her parents when they were both ill at the same time. She had then, in her late twenties, gone back to school to complete a degree but returned home to help her parents as her mother recovered from major emergency surgery and her father slowly died of Parkinson's disease. By the end of his illness, her father could no longer walk and was so depressed by his condition he would not talk.

Janet Spruce, only twenty-two years old, also worries about her parents' declining health and feels trapped, as the only child remaining at home, by their need of her. Her father, close to seventy and ailing, worries Janet by his unwillingness to help himself to greater strength: " . . . he really doesn't do much. He just kind of sits and eats and watches TV." Janet envies her sister who has left home and is "free." She feels her mother doesn't want the last child to leave home: "They feel older . . . she doesn't want to be left alone."

Some in the study, even though otherwise happy as children or for whom their parents' older years did not yet seem to present special burdens, had concerns as youngsters that their schoolmates seemed to be spared. Ted Martelli's father rarely participated in his son's life. "I never knew my father as a young man," Ted said. "He was retired when I was thirteen or fourteen . . . . Most of his life was lived before I was born. What I remember is him retiring." And Jim Compton, too, felt different from his friends in that his father, forty-four years old when Jim was born, retired from work when Jim was about fifteen and still in high school. "I was the only one whose father was retired . . . and that kinda worried me. You know, you retire and that's the end of your life, really . . . . [M]ost of my friends' fathers were just starting new jobs . . . something like that."

Both Jim and David Crenshaw were saddened that their fathers, unlike those of their friends, weren't able to participate in sports with them. They missed that. Jim was quick to add, though, that his parents, unlike some of the younger parents of his friends, were keen spectator supporters, attending all the games in which their son played. This, he felt, largely compensated for their inability to participate as players.

Older parents may be able to help their children face and overcome some of their special concerns and their fears about death, if they are, first, willing to acknowledge that late-parenting may have some detrimental effects on their children. Responses to an article on children of late-born children I wrote for the *Los Angeles Times* indicated a defensiveness by some late-starting parents, an inclination—perhaps naturally enough—to consider only the positive aspects of the maturity and the greater power to provide material things that added years bring. Some did not want late-parenting to be discussed at all, feeling that simply raising the subject turned it into a problem.

A recent study of ninety-eight expectant fathers in Greensborough, North Carolina, by Ora Strickland of the University of

Maryland, indicates that older expectant fathers (at least, those studied by Strickland) *are* concerned about their age and its effects on their offspring. The study shows that expectant fathers about thirty-five years old do worry about such things as whether they will be able to play basketball with their children or whether they will live long enough to see their children grow up. And, perhaps demonstrating the concerns over these issues in the society, a humorous depiction of them was given in one of the early Bill Cosby shows. Clair Huxtable, babysitting for a friend, falls in love with the helplessness and clean, sweet smell of the baby. Misty-eyed over having another bundle to love, she indicates her longing for another baby of her own. Cliff, her husband, tries to dissuade her. In his mid-forties, Cliff is realistic about his declining energy. He has just been beaten at basketball for the first time by his teenage son who recognizes that the reason his father so often pauses in the game to chat is so that he can regain his strength. Cliff, although understanding his wife's yearning, says of the "proposed" baby, "By the time that child leaves home, we'll be ready to *go* to one!"

Acknowledgment of these possibilities should help older people choosing to be parents to find alternative, less physically active ways of participating in their children's pursuits. As has been seen throughout this study of late-born children, youngsters greatly appreciate the *time* their parents spend with them. Those professing to happy childhood years all remember with joy the times spent with their parents. Those less happy as children regret their parents' absence from, to them, important aspects of their lives. An older man may not be able to play strenuous games but he can attend ballgames, can give support in other, equally valuable ways. Parents of any age can be involved in school activities, they can be welcoming to their children's friends, they can serve as sympathetic or emphathetic listeners and discussants. "I can always talk to my mother," Celia Abbott said, " 'cos, mostly, she just sits there and listens."

Fears of a parent's death are not easily discussed or dispelled. Few would advocate raising the issue and, perhaps, planting it in the mind of a child for whom it had not been a concern. Parents, though, can be alert to signs of worry. Marilyn Henry, parent of a late-born child and, herself, born late to her mother, is keenly aware that her only child, now seven years old, worries about her mother's death. This fear is exacerbated, Marilyn feels, by her own mother's recent death. "Mommy," the child asked, "did grandma have gray hair when you were my age?" Marilyn knows, she says, that the child is "trying to benchmark" events in the lives of her mother and grandmother so she can relate them to herself and her mother and assess when her mother, too, might die. Marilyn, acknowledging the child's fear, can be reassuring, emphasizing her grandmother's long life and that people now, knowing how to take better care of themselves, can be healthier and live even longer than did past generations.

The problem of presenting children with the responsibility of caring for their elderly and ailing parents while those children are still young and, perhaps, striving to establish their families and careers, is not simple to overcome. Few parents would choose to so burden their children, be those offspring in their thirties, or in their forties, fifties, or sixties, but, again, such a possibility, slight or otherwise, is probably better faced than ignored. It may belong in the same category of painful-to-discuss subjects as the inevitability of death and the need to write a will making clear one's preferences about funeral arrangements.

A summary of the advantages and disadvantages of late-parenting, as seen from the viewpoint of late-born children, shows a greater emphasis on its less favorable aspects than on its more favorable ones. Even the positive features of late-parenting listed were not seen as such by all the subjects, but neither did all the subjects perceive as disadvantages the items given under that heading.

What are the perceived advantages of being the child of older parents?

1. Older parents have more money, are more settled financially and, perhaps, emotionally, than younger parents.

While this was seen as beneficial for about half the sample of late-born children, including Charles Finch, Jim Compton, Janet Spruce, and Marilyn Henry, one subject, Margaret Pearce, saw it as a disadvantage, the expensive clothes her mother bought her emphasizing the existing difference between her and her friends. Another interviewee, Jean Smythe, disputed the notion that children know about, or care about, their parents' financial standing. " . . . a poor kid doesn't know he's poor," she said, "and a rich kid takes it for granted."

2. Older parents are wiser and more patient than younger parents, by virtue of having lived longer and experienced more.

Several late-born children felt their parents were wise, especially in their childrearing practices, This was especially so for Charles Finch, a caboose baby, who felt his parents had mellowed in the thirteen years between bringing up their first child and rearing Charles. His older sister was spanked more as a child than he was, his parents having learned from experience, he felt, that corporal punishment did not work well to improve children's behavior. Peter Cochran, an only child, was also eager to point out how much more wisdom and patience his parents brought to his upbringing than did the younger parents of his friends. His parents spent much more of their time before and after work with him, generous in sharing their considerable general and specific knowledge. Jim Cochran, a caboose baby, felt his childhood was happy largely due to the time and care his older parents devoted to him, and Alice Marshall, who started her own family late, feels her older parents were both wise. Parents who have their children late, she suggests, may feel less a sense of personal sacrifice when they have had childless years in which to enjoy and indulge themselves, and to gain some sense of their own talents and abilities.

Other subjects, though, did not perceive their older parents as especially wise or patient. Margaret Pearce and Barbara Anderson, both caboose babies, feel their parents' past experience of childrearing made them less rather than more interested in sharing their last child's activities. "If they had desires to do things with their children, they had already done them with their older children."

3. Parents' stability in their marriage.

The two high schoolers in the sample, Celia Abbott and Frank Martin, both appreciated their parents' marital stability. Said Celia, "Most of my friends, they have one parent, their parents are divorced. I have both my parents, even though they may be older." And Frank, although regretting the lack of communication between his parents and himself, was comforted by the fact of his parents' long-lasting marriage. "I feel they'll most probably stay together . . . I can feel . . . secure."

We cannot know, of course, whether those choosing late-parenting now will have marriages as stable as those of most of the parents of the people interviewed for this study. It cannot be overlooked, too, that Peter Cochran's parents did divorce when Peter was twenty years old, and Rebecca Johnson's parents were divorced when Rebecca was about seven. They remarried later, but their marriage seems to have been somewhat turbulent.

What are the perceived disadvantages of being the child of older parents?

1. Older parents are less energetic than younger parents, less able to be physically active.
2. Parents whose children are born late in their lives are likely to be afflicted with the problems of old age when their children are not yet middle-aged.

3. Older parents are less likely to live to see their children reach adulthood. Fathers, especially, are more likely to die when their offspring are in their teens, or even younger.
4. Late-parenting brings a double generation gap in understanding between the parents and their children. Older parents "forget what it is like" to be young and newly aware of one's sexuality.
5. Older parents may be an embarrassment to their children because their physical appearance makes them stand out from younger parents.
6. Because older parents are, to some extent, like grandparents, children may find it difficult to "rebel" against them in ways that are considered normal in our culture.

Some of these perceived disadvantages may seem trivial, especially to those who are not, themselves, children of older parents; others are less easy to dismiss. But it could properly be argued that *all* children feel deprived in some ways and that the adult who can find no fault at all with his parents' childrearing practices does not exist. Every child feels lonely, frightened, unloved, and misunderstood at times, and the need for the kind of support from parents that encourages a strong sense of self-worth, of importance to others, exists for all youngsters, regardless of their parents' ages.

These perceptions, though, trivial or otherwise, of the advantages and disadvantages of late-parenting from the viewpoint of late-born children, are real and important to the perceivers. As W. I. Thomas, the sociologist-philosopher, expressed it: "If men define situations as real, they are real in their consequences." Many of the late-born children interviewed for the study believed themselves disadvantaged by being born to older parents, these beliefs helping to color their view of the world and of themselves.

Our pictures of ourselves and our place in our society depend largely upon, and are reinforced by, the ways others, especially significant others, respond to us. The results of several studies indicate that self-concept and feelings of self-worth grow and change in interaction with others who are important to us. Robert Rosenthal and Lenore Jacobson's classroom study, for instance, illustrates how children see images of themselves reflected in the eyes of their teachers.

Children expected by their teachers to make greater intellectual gains than other children of similar intelligence, did make such gains. Although the teachers insisted they had spent no more time with the "spurters" than with the other children, the "experimental children" appear to have perceived themselves as special, as favored, and responded accordingly. Teachers are of considerable significance in children's lives, especially for young children (the intellecual gains were greater in grades one and two than in grades three through six) and the study indicates that a child's self-perception can be strongly affected by the views and expectations of others important to him or her.

Another classroom experiment, conducted by Jane Elliott and later reenacted in *The Eye of the Storm*, a television documentary, again showed the powerful influence on a child's self-concept of the opinion of an admired teacher and friends and other classmates. Jane Elliott, whose third-grade class was in a school in the rural Midwest, far from the turbulence of a multiethnic, multiracial city, found a way of demonstrating the nature of prejudice for her all-white pupils. She discriminated first against blue-eyed children and then against brown-eyed children by praising the favored group and emphasizing the "weaknesses" of the shunned group. In each case, the disparaged, discredited children soon became listless, withdrawn, and unhappy and began performing their lessons badly, demonstrating that if people are seen by others as "different" in a negative way, or as strange or less valuable than those around them, they will soon perceive themselves in the same way and act to reinforce that view. If children are teased about their parents, if their parents are mistaken for grandparents and disparaged as old, or if attitudes are perceived as disparaging even if that was not the intention, they can, as did some of the now grown late-born children in this study, feel hurt and shame for their parents and ultimately, for themselves.

Some children, though, are less deeply affected by the views of outsiders and seem able to retain a strong, positive sense of self even against assaults by others. One small boy in Jane Elliott's third-grade classroom refused to accept the discriminatory statements and actions of the teacher and his classmates; he remained openly skeptical—even disdainful—of suggestions that eye color made a difference to a person's worth or intelligence, while other children appeared to accept them without question. Throughout, this little boy remained in firm possession of his sense of self.

Some social psychologists and other social scientists maintain that this kind of sense of worth, giving one power to resist and withstand undermining influences, is developed early in life from positive, accepting interaction with those caregivers of greatest significance to the child. Armentrout and Burger (1972), for instance, have found that warm, nurturing parents help a child achieve independence and security in his or her relations with others. On the other hand, according to R. Rohner (1975), children who have cool or inattentive parents are more likely than other children to lack social skills. Several of the late-born children in this study who remember their childhood years as happy and rewarding were treated by their parents as valuable, important, and capable people. These include Charles Finch, Peter Cochran, and Priscilla Banks, none of whom were especially aware that their parents' ages made them different from the parents of their classmates. Their strong sense of themselves seems to have protected them from negative outside influences.

What steps can older parents take to help their children lead relatively happy, untroubled lives? Children of older parents give their suggestions.

While only a few of the late-born children interviewed said they would choose late parenting for themselves, or recommend it as a pattern for others, several did offer some ideas about how the childhood happiness of late-born children might be enhanced.

Cheryl Greenham, speaking from her experience as a teacher as well as a late-born child, feels it is vital for parents to develop an extra rapport with children when there is a substantial age gap. The issues, both negative and positive, of a double generation gap between parents and child should be faced and discussed, she said. If she has children in her late thirties, she plans, too, to have more fun with them than her parents had with her and, given her mother's history of debilitatingly poor health, she considers a fitness program a priority for older parents. To have teenage children when one is into one's fifties is, for Cheryl, "cause to try and stay as fit and healthy as you can."

Charles Finch, who remembers his childhood fondly, feels his mother and father provide excellent models of parenthood. They clearly welcomed their late-born son, took time to enjoy him and, because they were financially comfortable by their middle years, were able to indulge him materially more than would have been possible in their younger days. His parents had mellowed over the years, he feels, and were wise enough to provide comforts and pleasures without spoiling him. They were also able to instill discipline and commitment to learning in him while rarely resorting to physical punishment. Charles feels material things are important to children and, as older parents are more likely to be established financially than are younger ones, age can be a positive asset to parenting.

Marilyn Henry, too, who did make the choice to have her first, and only, child relatively late, feels that children benefit from their parents' ability to buy whatever is felt necessary, without a too careful counting of pennies. Because of her own experience as a late-born child, she also recognizes her child's special need for careful reassurances about her parents' mortality. Rather than dismiss or ignore the questions, she feels it is important to address the late-born child's concerns about death openly and positively to relieve or dispel his or her fears.

Peter Cochran, whose parents spent all their free time with him, feels, as does Charles Finch, that his mother and father provided a fine pattern of parenting, a pattern he hopes to emulate, with some variations, when he has children of his own. He does not expect to become a father until well into his thirties; he believes that parents should devote time to their children and the early years of struggle to establish himself in his career would preclude that. For Peter, parental attention is both precious and vital to a child's development and contentment although he feels that the close, even closed, circle of mother, father, and child can be confining. Parents, he suggests, while giving much of themselves to their offspring, should make sure their children have a broader range of contacts, including other adults.

Teenager Frank Martin, another of the few who might, he said, wait until late, until he is thirty-five, before he starts his family, says "I would talk to [my children] more. I would praise them. I would communicate with them more." The requirement of time spent with their children is repeated over and over again in the recommendations to older mothers and fathers by now-adult children of such parents. Meg Perkins gives this advice to any parents, no matter what their age: "I think the difference between a kid being happy or not has to do with parents being able to spend a lot of good, quality time with the kid." Children, she feels, as does Peter Cochran and others in the sample, "need other people of *all* ages."

Jim Cochran, feeling himself fortunate in having a devoted older sister as well as attentive parents, found the time his parents spent with him helped significantly to overcome the drawbacks of being a late-born child. His parents, although both worked outside the home, had working hours that allowed them to be present at school games to cheer their son from the sidelines. They also enjoyed board games at home with the family; these kinds of activities, Jim maintains, gave him a feeling of stability and security.

Ted Martelli was at first unwilling to view late-parenting in any positive way. Although he recognized the sense of purpose that children bring to their parents' lives, he felt that having children was not necessarily a healthy way to energize one's later life. He conceded, though, that if at his present age of forty-six he had not yet had children, he might feel differently. As a child-oriented person, he sees children as essential to his life and would certainly have wanted to have them. If he were to advise older people about childrearing, the first essential he would emphasize is that they spend time with their children. Like most of the other respondents in this study, he felt that "children need and want parents' time." Ted Martelli's sentiments were supported by Margaret Pearce, whose childhood, she feels, lacked the kind of parental attention she tries to provide for her own children. "If you're not willing to give your time and attention to your children then you're not giving either yourself or your child a fair chance." And Rebecca Johnson further added that having children is a lifetime commitment that potential parents should be sure they want to undertake. Alice Marshall, too, feels strongly that parents, mothers especially, need to bond with their children so that task must come before all others, especially when the children are young.

Final Words

The idea that a child should be "the main thing" to its parents was voiced by a number of the children of older parents, raising the question that plagues and perplexes many women who have delayed parenting while they complete their formal education and establish themselves in their careers. Women today are led to expect that they can "have it all"—careers, marriage, and motherhood—and they believe they can easily accommodate children to their existing careers. But, as the NBC whitepaper, "Women, Work, and Babies," indicated, and as is supported both by the complaints of women who are attempting it and by social scientists studying it (see Piotrkowski 1979; Rapoport and Rapoport 1976), and as is further demonstrated by the University of California and other schools who now offer extension courses for people in need of help in "doing-it-all," juggling career and family is difficult indeed. So exhausting and demanding is the exercise that the quality of many marriages suffers as, according to some reports, does the sense of security of the children involved.

Within the academic literature on child care, research findings are so contradictory that sufficient "evidence" can be found to support any point of view about working parents and their responsibilities to their children. The child developmentalist Burton White is adamant that children need and should have the loving care of a consistent care-giver, preferably a parent, for the first several years of their lives if they are to develop as emotionally healthy adults. The equally respected Jerome Kagan of Harvard, on the other hand, claims this to be something of a myth. Children, Kagan says, fare as well in day care as at home with a parent but the day care, he insists, must be of high quality, with well-trained care-givers in attendance.

As is well known to parents who need it, however, high quality day care is a scarce, high-costing commodity in many parts of the United States at present. Day-care options are few and many working parents, according to "Women, Work, and Babies," among other sources, find themselves beset with guilt as they leave their children with various kinds of child-minders and proceed to their jobs.

This study of late-born children is not intended to exacerbate career women's existing anxieties about combining work and babies, but the responses of now-adult children born late in their parents' lives do indicate the need such children— perhaps all children—feel for attention from their parents.

One of the most important factors making for perceived happiness in the lives of late-born children appears to be the time their parents spend with them. And the most insistent plea from those late-born children who were not happy, or who were less happy, in their childhood years is for parents to spend more time with their offspring, to be more aware of children's need for attention from those who mean more to them than anyone else in their world.

We hear much about working parents spending "quality time" with their children but the children in this study wanted, and some received, *quantities* of their parents' time, that time devoted to the children's needs and interests, to building in their children a sturdy, resilient sense of self-worth, security, and stability. Burton White uses the word positively when he speaks of parents and grandparents as having an "irrational" interest in the normal developmental activities of their children and grandchildren. Children thrive on the glowing, unqualified, "irrational" approval of their simplest achievements.

An enormous literature, both popular and technical, is devoted to pregnancy and delivery—those nine months of change and drama. Compared, though, to the years that parents are responsbile for their children's well-being, pregnancy is brief and infancy is fleeting. It may be that, in contemplating parenthood, few of us, in our twenties or in our thirties and forties, think beyond pregnancy and, then, holding a baby in our arms.

Margaret Pearce's mother, her youngest child then close to her teens, reportedly decided to have another child after caring for a relative's newborn. "It's very nice, holding a baby again," she said to her husband, " ... this is our last chance." Her enthusiasm and interest, according to Margaret, diminished as her baby became a child and, then, a teenager. Barbara Anderson, another less than happy child, recalls that her mother did pay attention to her at one time. "I remember quite distinctly, when I was three or four, before I started school, my mother would sit me on her lap and we would read the newspaper and she would make me read the article out loud. And if there was a word I didn't know or couldn't pronounce, we'd circle it and go back to it ... My mother recently wrote me about how, when I was a baby, she would carry me around the museum, and we were physically close, and she felt so good having me, and said I would point at things and she would explain them to me, and there was this very loving relationship." That closeness, that holding and sharing, did not continue.

For career men and women, for whom time is their most valuable and their scarcest commodity, finding time—and energy—to give to their children may mean a reordering of priorities and the sacrifice of some once-enjoyed aspects of their lives, not only during the important early years of their children's development but also during their pre-teens and adolescence. For those parents for whom these sacrifices would mean the end, or the shunting into a siding, of a promising career or the impossibility of surviving economically, possible alternatives include the finding of nurturing substitute parents or grandparents with whom their children can feel emotionally close and safe until their parents can be with them.

Women today who are contemplating starting families in their mid to late thirties and their forties are, as a group, among the brightest, most highly educated, most professionally well-trained, and financially the most comfortable ever to embark on this venture. What is more, they truly want babies; they have waited for them for a long time and look forward to their arrival with joyous anticipation. But, while children appear to many to be the final feather in the cap of achievement, the ultimate fulfillment of biological and emotional needs, the tie that bonds a compatible couple, children bring with them their own needs and priorities, their own demands that change irrevocably their parents' way of life.

The now-adult children of older parents who have spoken out here speak from their own experiences, from the pleasure and the pain they felt—and still feel—about some aspects of their family lives. They show that the relationship between older parents and their children can be happy and enriching; they also show that late-born children may have problems not confronted by children with younger parents. Theirs is a voice not heard before. The stories they tell can raise the awareness of older parents, and those contemplating late-parenting, to their children's concerns; their suggestions can begin to provide some common-sense solutions to those concerns.

References

Armentrout, V. A. and G. K. Burger. "Children's Reports of Parental Child-rearing Behaviors at Five Grade Levels." *Developmental Psychology* (1972) 7:44-48

"At Long Last Motherhood." *Newsweek,* March 16, 1981.

Bing. Elizabeth and Libby Colman. *Having a Baby After Thirty.* New York: Bantam Books, 1980.

Brislin, R. et al. *Cross-Cultural Perspectives on Learning.* New York: Halsted Press, 1975.

Boston Women's Health Book Collective. *Our Bodies, Our Selves.* New York: Simon and Schuster, 1976.

Bronfenbrenner, Urie. "Who Cares for America's Children?" Paper presented at the annual meeting of the National Association for the Education of Young Children. 1970. Cited in Zigler and Finn-Stevenson, *Children: Development and Policy* p. 57.

Cizmar, Paula L. "Aunt Mary Said There'd Be Days Like This." *Mother Jones* (February/March 1979), pp. 21-30.

Clarke-Stewart, Alison. *Daycare.* Cambridge, Mass: Harvard University Press, 1982.

Clarke-Stewart, Alison and Joanne Barbara Koch. *Children: Development Through Adolescence.* New York: Wiley, 1983.

Clarke-Stewart, Alison, Susan Friedman, and Joanne Koch. *Child Development: A Topical Approach.* New York: Wiley, 1985.

Daniels, Pamela and Kathy Weingarten. "A New Look at Medical Risks in Late Childbearing." *Women and Health* (Spring 1979), pp. 17-21.

Daniels, Pamela and Kathy Weingarten. *Sooner or Later: The Timing of Parenthood in Adult Lives.* New York: Norton, 1982.

Doyle, A-B. "Infant Development in Daycare." *Developmental Psychology* (1975), 11:655-656.

Dullea, Georgia. "When Motherhood Doesn't Mean Marriage." *New York Times*, November 26, (1978), p. 28.

Ephron, Nora. "Having a Baby After 35." *New York Times Magazine*, November 26, 1978, p. 28.

Fabe, Marilyn and Norma Wikler. *Up Against the Clock: Career Women Speak on the Choice to Have Children*. New York: Random House, 1979.

Falbo, Toni, ed. *The Single Child Family*. New York: Guilford Press, 1984.

Fuller, Doris Byron. "Baby Boom Puts Style on Bottom Line." *Los Angeles Times*, September 8, 1983.

Glaser, Barney G. and Anselm Strauss. *The Discovery of Grounded Theory: Strategies for Qualitative Reseach*. Chicago: Aldine, 1967.

Goffman, Erving. *Stigma: Notes on the Management of Spoiled Identity* Englewood Cliffs, N.J.: Prentice Hall, 1963.

Golbus, Mitchell S. and Associates. "Prenatal Genetic Diagnosis in 3000 Amniocenteses." *New England Journal of Medicine*, January 25, 1979.

Grout, H. Theodore, Jerry W. Wicks, and Arthur G. Neal. "Without Siblings: The Consequences in Adult Life of Having Been an Only Child." In Falbo, ed., *The Single Child Family*, pp. 253-289.

Hawke, Sharryl and David Knox. *One Child by Choice*. Englewood Cliffs, N.J.: Prentice Hall, 1977.

Holmes, Lewis B. "Genetic Counseling for the Older Pregnant Woman: New Data and Questions." *New England Journal of Medicine*, June 22, 1978.

Jones, Landon Y. *Great Expectations: America and the Baby Boom Generation*. New York: Ballantine Books, 1981.

Kagan, Jerome. *The Nature of the Child*. New York: Basic Books, 1984.

Kagan, J., R. B. Kearsley, and P. R. Zalazo. *Infancy: Its Place in Human Development*. Cambridge, Mass.: Harvard University Press, 1978.

Kappelman, Murray, M.D. *Raising the Only Child*. New York: Dutton, 1975

Klemesrud, Judy, "Single Mothers by Choice: Perils and Joys." *New York Times*, May 2, 1983, p. B5.

Kornhaber, A. and K. L. Woodward. *Grandparents/Grandchildren: The Vital Connection*. Garden City, N.Y: Anchor Press, 1981.

Leopold, Wendy. "Mid-Life Soul Searching With the '39- and Holding' Crowd." *Los Angeles Times*. View. February 20, 1987.

Lamb, M.E. and B. Sutton Smith, eds. *Sibling Relationships: Their Nature and Significance across the Life Span*. Hillside, N.J.: Erlbaum, 1982.

Lindsey, Robert. "Experts Anticipating Bit of a Baby Boom This Year." *New York Times*, September 2, 1980.

McCauley, Carole. *Pregnancy After 35*. New York: Dutton, 1976

McFeatters, Ann. "Toppling Myths of Older Mothers." *Los Angeles Times*, December 4, 1983, *View* section, p. 17.

Morris, Monica. "Children of Older Mothers and Fathers Face Special Challenges." *Los Angeles Times*, March 28, 1984.

Morris, Monica B. *An Excursion Into Creative Sociology.* New York: Columbia University Press, 1977.

Munson, Naomi. "Having Babies Again." *Commentary,* (April 1981), 71(4):60-63.

Mussen, Paul Henry, John Janeway Conger, and Jerome Kagan. *Child Development and Personality.* New York: Harper and Row, 1969

Norment, Lynn. "Should Women Have Babies After 35?" *Ebony,* July 1981.

Orwell, George. "Such, such were the joys . . . " in *A Collection of Essays.* New York: Doubleday, 1954.

Parachini, Allan. "Over 35 Pregnancy No Longer Termed 'Risky'." *Los Angeles Times,* View, March 25, 1986, p. 1.

Peck, Ellen. *The Joy of the Only Child.* New York: Delacorte Press, 1975.

Pepler, Debra. "Naturalistic Observations of Teaching and Modeling between Siblings." Paper presented at the biennial meeting of the Society for Research in Child Development. Boston. 1981.

Peters, William. *A Class Divided.* New York: Doubleday, 1971.

Piotrkowski, C. S. *Work and the Family System: A Naturalistic Study of Working Class and Lower-Middle Class Families.* New York: Free Press, 1979.

Price, Jane. *You're Not Too Old to Have a Baby.* New York: Farrar, Strauss and Giroux, 1977.

Rapoport, Rhona, Robert N. Rapoport, and Ziona Stelitz. *Fathers, Mothers, and Society.* New York: Basic Books, 1977.

Rapoport, Robert and Rhona Rapoport. *Dual Career Families Revisited: New Generations of Work and Family.* New York: Harper Colophon, 1976.

Robertson, J. F. "Significance of grandparents: perceptions of young adult grandchildren." *The Gerontologist.* (1976), 16:137-140.

Rohner, R. "Parental Acceptance-Rejection and Personality: A Universal Approach to Behavioral Science." Cited in Zigler and Finn-Stevenson, *Children: Development and Social Issues,* p. 557.

Rosenthal, Robert, and Lenore Jacobson. "Teachers' Expectancies: Determinants of Pupils' IQ Gains." *Psychological Reports* (1966) 19:115-118.

Salisbury, Arthur J. M.D. Letter to *Commentary.,* September 1981, p. 18.

Schaffer, H. R. and P. E. Emerson. "The Development of Social Attachments in Infancy." Cited in Clark-Stewart, Friedman, and Koch; *Child Development.* p. 461.

Schulz, Terri. *Women Can Wait.* Garden City, N.Y.: Doubleday, 1979.

Sklar, June and Beth Berkov. "The American Birthrate: Evidence of a Coming Rise." *Science,* August 29, 1975.

Sontag, Susan. "The Double Standard of Aging." *Saturday Review,* September 23, 1972.

Spiegel, Lise. "Childbirth Over 40." *Harper's Bazaar,* September 1981.

Sunila, Joyce. "A Love Nearly Missed." *Reader's Digest,* May 1984, pp. 21-28.

United States Department of Commerce, Bureau of the Census. Current Population Reports. Population characteristics.
"Fertility of American Women: June 1982." Series P-20, No. 379, May 1983.
　"Fertility of American Women: June 1981." Series P-20, No 378, May 1982.
　Statistical Abstract of the United States, 1982-1983. Washington, D.C.: GPO, 1983.
Wakerman, Elyce. *Father Loss: Women Discuss the Man That Got Away.* New York: Doubleday, 1984.
Warshaw, Robin. "The American Way of Birth." *Ms.* Magazine, September 1984.
Whelan, Elizabeth. *A Baby? . . . Maybe.* New York: Bobbs-Merrill, 1975.
White, Burton L. *The First Three Years of Life.* Englewood Cliffs, N.J.: Prentice Hall, 1975.
Wolfe, Linda. "The Coming Baby Boom." *New York Magazine,* January 10, 1977, pp. 40-41.
"Women, Work, and Babies." NBC Whitepaper. Aired in Los Angeles March 16, 1985.
Yarrow, Andrew L. "Older Parents' Child: Growing Up Special." *New York Times,* Style, January 26, 1987.
Zigler, Edward F. and Matia Finn-Stevenson. *Children: Development and Social Issues.* Lexington, Mass.: D.C. Heath, 1987.